Jossey-Bass Teacher

Jossey-Bass Teacher provides K–12 teachers with essential knowledge and tools to create a positive and lifelong impact on student learning. Trusted and experienced educational mentors offer practical classroom-tested and theory-based teaching resources for improving teaching practice in a broad range of grade levels and subject areas. From one educator to another, we want to be your first source to make every day your best day in teaching. *Jossey-Bass Teacher* resources serve two types of informational needs—essential knowledge and essential tools.

Essential knowledge resources provide the foundation, strategies, and methods from which teachers may design curriculum and instruction to challenge and excite their students. Connecting theory to practice, essential knowledge books rely on a solid research base and time-tested methods, offering the best ideas and guidance from many of the most experienced and well-respected experts in the field.

Essential tools save teachers time and effort by offering proven, ready-to-use materials for in-class use. Our publications include activities, assessments, exercises, instruments, games, ready reference, and more. They enhance an entire course of study, a weekly lesson, or a daily plan. These essential tools provide insightful, practical, and comprehensive materials on topics that matter most to K–12 teachers.

Partners in Crime

PARTNERS in CRIME

INTEGRATING LANGUAGE ARTS AND FORENSIC SCIENCE, GRADES 5-8

E.K. HEIN

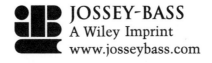

JOSSEY-BASS
A Wiley Imprint
www.josseybass.com

Published by Jossey-Bass
A Wiley Imprint
989 Market Street, San Francisco, CA 94103-1741   www.josseybass.com

Jossey-Bass books and products are available through most bookstores. To contact Jossey-Bass directly call our Customer Care Department within the U.S. at 800-956-7739, outside the U.S. at 317-572-3986, or fax 317-572-4002.

Jossey-Bass also publishes its books in a variety of electronic formats. Some content that appears in print may not be available in electronic books.

Library of Congress Cataloging-in-Publication Data
Hein, E. K., date.
  Partners in crime : integrating language arts and forensic science, grades 5-8 / E.K. Hein.— 1st ed.
    p. cm.
  Includes bibliographical references.
  ISBN 0-7879-6993-1 (alk. paper)
  1. Forensic sciences—Study and teaching—United States. 2. Language arts (Secondary)—United States. 3. Interdisciplinary approach in education—United States. I. Title: Integrating language arts and forensic science, grades 5-8. II. Title.
  HV8073.H345 2004
  363.25'071'273—dc22
                                                                                    2004014538

Printed in the United States of America
FIRST EDITION
PB Printing   10 9 8 7 6 5 4 3 2 1

About This Book

Why This Topic Is Important

Teachers need a variety of approaches to instruction as well as a variety of high-interest lessons for their classes. In a compelling coupling of language arts and forensic science inquiry, *Partners in Crime* offers a comprehensive, thematically linked format of units, lesson plans, activities, and exercises within the context of a ready-to-use format. Through the contribution of the school community and its resources, the use of technology, and student participation, this title supports the middle school concept of thematic, interdisciplinary team building. Ultimately, the goal of this book is to keep students engaged and interested as they learn key concepts and skills related to language arts.

What You Can Achieve with This Book

Partners in Crime gives you activities and benchmarks throughout in order to meet the goal of standards-based learning. There are also overt connections to real-world methods of information gathering, realia (such as caution tape, official forms, and evidence collection items), as well as suggestions for connections to local law enforcement support to provide students with a method to help them make meaning of their studies. The exercises in this book encourage students to conduct original research, while challenging them to draw conclusions that are based upon their ability to weigh evidence. Units culminate in thorough written reports, presentations, and even opportunities for film and video. You are encouraged to use this book to invigorate your classrooms, as you offer your students an innovative, high-interest, standards-conforming curriculum.

How This Book Is Organized

These elements are in each of the fifteen chapters:

- Teacher materials:
  Overview (for teacher background; grade-level appropriateness, key or code to learning modalities)
  Introduction to subject matter (for teacher; to be read to students)
  Vocabulary

Lesson objectives (with standards "guide words")

Assessment

Lesson accommodations and modifications (for ESL, English as a second language)

For further study

References

- Student materials:

Lessons and learning activities

Exercises

Instruments

Games

Ready references

Springboards to writing

About the Author

E. K. Hein is a middle school language arts teacher in the suburbs of Philadelphia. He resides in the town of Jeffersonville with his wife, Karina, and his son, Lukas. Having taught language arts and English skills to students for eight years, he was drawn to the notion of a thematic, interdisciplinary unit involving crime scene investigations when his "partner in crime," Pamela Gray, a science teacher, bought him a copy of William Maples's *Dead Men Do Tell Tales*. He subsequently became an avid reader of forensic nonfiction, as well as an attendant of various special seminars at the Virginia Institute of Forensic Science and Medicine, and at the American Academy of Forensic Science, which is designed for teachers to explore modern crime-fighting techniques and apply them in a classroom setting. He spent a summer working at the Forensic Mentor Institute, at which he led high school students in original research that was presented at the annual convention for the American Chemical Society. He has also presented with Pam Gray at the Pennsylvania Middle Schools Association and the National Science Teachers Association. He also wrote and received a $10,000 grant from the Toyota Tapestry fund to provide his students with real crime-scene equipment to use in class. In 2003, his "Investigating Crime Scenes in Literature" was featured in the *Wall Street Journal* as a model for innovative, engaging curriculum. He also published an article about his project in the April 2004 edition of the National Council of Teachers of English *Classroom Notes Plus*. Through his passion and dedication to education and the pursuit of justice, he challenges his students every day with inquiry-based problems and higher-level thinking skills. He was also named a member of the Educator 500 program through West Chester University.

For Karina, my partner in life,
and Pamela Gray, my partner in crime

Acknowledgments

CRIME SCENE DO NOT CROSS CRIME SCENE DO NOT CROSS CRIME SCENE DO NOT CROSS CRIME SCENE DO NOT CROSS CRIME SCENE DO NOT CROSS CRIME SCENE DO NOT CROSS CRIME SCENE DO NOT CROSS

First, I would like to thank my partner in crime and mentor, Pamela Gray. Without her, this book would not be. Special thanks to my wife, Karina; and to Mom and Dad for your help and putting up with my experiments. Also, thank you, Kathleen Conn, for all of your help and support; and you, Cathie White, for your advice and guidance. I would also like to thank Sgt. William Cahill, Leo Kennedy, Steve Wassell, Glen Bretz, Mike Ragney, Bob Balchnus, the Westtown East Goshen Police Department, Cheryl Custard, and Assistant District Attorney Renee Merion; the kids really enjoy having you come in to speak to them. Finally, my thanks go to the Virginia Institute of Forensic Science and Medicine, the Frederic Rieders Family Renaissance Foundation, Frederic Rieders, John DiGregorio, Jim Hurley, the American Academy of Forensic Science, and the students and mentors at the Forensic Mentor Institute.

Contents

Letter to the Reader

To My Fellow Language Arts and Science Teachers:

Relevance of subject matter to the lives of our students plays a significant role in education, especially in middle school. This project capitalizes on the current popularity of such media phenomena as TV's *CSI* series and uses forensic science as a vehicle to integrate language arts and science. By stressing reading in the content area and addressing different learning styles, this book aims to elevate literacy and student achievement. Through standards-based activities, you, the teacher, will find this book the perfect avenue to meet standards and incorporate higher-level thinking, which will result in higher test scores.

Social skills are also developed through cooperative learning, a term that is slowly fading as schools constantly struggle to meet the requirements of the No Child Left Behind Act. By integrating existing curriculum within English and science curricula, teachers have an ideal opportunity to collaborate and display to students that core subjects in fact do cross over from one to the other. Yes, time is precious in our busy and industrious lives, but a quick meeting in the hallway while your students are shuffling into class or while you are walking to your car at the end of the day accomplishes a lot.

Although this book contains a copious amount of science background, it also ties in the necessity of language arts skills to solve crimes. These essential elements of language arts help students make evaluations and analyze information in a way that applies to the practicality of life and the standardized tests students face several times throughout the year. Because it does involve a high level of interest, students develop a desire to read more. You will also see new relationships develop with other students. They will be actively engaged in conversation in and out of the classroom. Soon word travels, and students are excited about coming to class.

Other relationships are developed with the members of the law enforcement community. This is very important because typical middle school students do not look at law enforcement as a close friend. Students learn that those professionals are just as normal as they are, and even share some of the same interests. Students will approach them outside of school and engage in conversation about solving crimes.

As you begin reading through this book, you will be embarking on a new experience that is rewarding and educational for both you and your students. The science background provides a basic framework of knowledge a teacher can build upon. As you begin to involve outside authorities, motivation will grow (for you and your students). This book is a terrific segue to integrating curricula, developing new relationships, meeting standards, promoting social awareness, and raising test scores.

Sincerely,
E. K. Hein

Partners in Crime

Introduction

Interviewing, Information Gathering, and Global Concerns

Overview for Teachers

This book offers many suggestions regarding how you may incorporate the study of forensic science into a typical middle school language arts classroom. Although this book and the suggestions contained herein do not require any formal training in forensic science, *Partners in Crime* is meant to give you alternatives and options that may reinvigorate instruction through a thoughtful and constructivist approach. I have found that the best way to get kids involved with this type of inquiry is to make lessons as hands-on as possible. Furthermore, connecting new knowledge in these lessons with real resources from the community, including law enforcement officers and other forensics professionals, is the key to the success of this material. Officials are often pleased and more than willing to assist in the classroom and also furnish materials for labs. My intention is not to remake a language arts curriculum; instead, I would like to offer the ideas in this book as a suggestion to you to enhance certain curricular units and to supplement instruction with a fun and innovative set of strategies. The rest of the introduction lays out one way for you to consider starting with this book. The lessons deal with interviewing and information gathering, and they are presented in the same fashion as all of the thematic lessons in the following chapters.

Community Resources

Using the local community is an important component of this project. Ideally, authorities will establish a working relationship with students throughout the year. I have found that it is best for you to make contacts in the beginning of the year, to establish visitation times and the names of people coming to the

2 **Introduction**

CRIME SCENE DO NOT CROSS CRIME SCENE DO NOT CROSS CRIME SCENE DO NOT CROSS CRIME SCENE DO NOT CROSS CRIME SCENE DO NOT CROSS CRIME SCENE DO NOT CROSS CRIME SCENE

school. It is important to plan ahead! I have learned that it is best to think in terms of a three-to-four-month lead time for securing the participation of law enforcement professionals from the community in your classroom activities. With other officials it may take longer or shorter to acquire their time, depending on availability.

The goal, of course, is to give students the opportunity to practice with interview subjects in the immediate environment first (teachers, families, and other students) and then encourage them to venture forth into settings where they are able to practice their skills. Ultimately, this may lead students to career exploration, but the purpose of this book is to foster a desire to practice and learn various language arts skills in the context of an exciting and popular framework.

General Guidelines for Community Visits

Once you are able to secure a visit from local community officials, the first visit should consist of an informal session where a police officer may discuss his or her daily responsibilities and duties. The officer should also explain the various areas of law enforcement. Some departments have a detectives unit, a road patrol unit, officers on bikes, accident units, and task forces of narcotics officers. Programs that are in place to assist the community as well as students in school should also be discussed. Most departments have a DARE (Drug Abuse Resistance Education) officer who is willing to get involved with the students too. Outside of the police department, officers sometimes use other agencies, including the FBI. These areas can be tapped as well. Students should be encouraged to ask questions to develop a comfortable relationship with the officer. The ultimate goal is to have students feel safe and comfortable with speaking to the officer openly.

Involving the Authorities and Experts

One overall teaching goal for the thematic units in this book is for students to be able to use resources that they have on hand, whether source texts, physical evidence, or testimony. Students will be exploring interviewing skills with various informants: the teacher, other students, and a professional law enforcement officer. Throughout the interviewing process (which may be somewhat daunting), it is incumbent for the interviewer to begin with the end in mind. In other words, the interviewer should always have a sense of generally what sort of information he or she would like to glean from the interviewee. In the end, the goal is to teach students how to feel at ease when conducting an interview.

It is important for students to conduct preliminary research prior to conducting an interview. They should know some of the relative strengths and weaknesses of their informants, and they should always begin the interview process with a thorough list of questions that they plan to ask. Although there is a certain art to questioning strategy, the simple science of it involves asking divergent (open-ended) instead of convergent (closed-ended) questions. Students should pay particular attention to the quality of information they are receiving from a respondent. Throughout, students should make note of the importance and involvement that the interviewee will play in the respective field or area of expertise.

An easy way to get students involved is to place the questions given here on an index card. As students enter the room, you can randomly pass out cards to students as they come through the door.

Possible Interview Questions and Format

Through this question-and-answer period, students will feel comfortable with asking the officer all kinds of questions. Remind students beforehand to save their "what if" questions until the end. This way, the officer can explain his or her basic responsibilities.

Some sample questions to ask a prospective volunteer:

Why did you choose to become a police officer?

What do you like about your job?

What do you not like about your job?

What was your most frightening moment as a police officer?

What is your fondest memory of your job?

How do you deal with tough moments in your job?

How can you resolve a conflict without anyone getting hurt?

What role do the media play in some of your investigations?

What kind of training do you need to become a police officer?

What are your hobbies and interests?

These are basic questions that get the officer talking and students thinking. This activity can be done with various members in the field. Do not hesitate to invite the local coroner or an emergency medical technician into the classroom to explain the role he or she plays in solving crimes. There are plenty of opportunities in future chapters to invite an array of community members into the classroom.

Explanation to the students requires organization. They must first understand that this is a cross-curriculum activity. Students are being asked to transfer information from one class to another. Throughout the year, people from the police department, forensic scientists, and other members of the community will visit students. Also, group work is required for labs in science as well as other classes. This promotes positive social development skills.

Introduction to Subject Matter

Interviewing someone is not an easy task. The interviewer needs to know what kind of questions to ask in order to get the information that is valuable. Journalists and other members of the broadcasting and news reporting community need interviewing skills to

4   **Introduction**

CRIME SCENE DO NOT CROSS CRIME SCENE DO NOT CROSS CRIME SCENE DO NOT CROSS CRIME SCENE DO NOT CROSS CRIME SCENE DO NOT CROSS CRIME SCENE DO NOT CROSS CRIME SCENE

survive in the media world. A good interviewer focuses on a topic and develops questions that are directly related to the story being written or reported. It is just like gathering ideas for a paper or a project. Develop preliminary questions first and review them to ensure they are focused on the topic. Anything not related is useless and time consuming.

Put students in groups of two (divide the total number of students in your class by two, and count off by rows so two students have a corresponding number). Those students are partners. If you have an odd number of students, have a group of three. When they get into groups, have them answer the questions given here. They should be posted on the board for the class to see. Have one student record the answers on a single sheet of paper.

> If a reporter were to interview a sports player, what kind of questions would be important?
>
> What about a CEO of a big corporation?
>
> A sanitation worker for the city?
>
> Now think about why a general set of questions cannot be developed for this purpose. Why must the questions be more detailed and specific?
>
> What if journalists and reporters used the same questions for all people?

Give students approximately six to eight minutes to complete the task. Then go over the answers orally and generate a list on the board.

General Vocabulary

Law enforcement	Any member of a police organization that deals with the laws governing a country
Homicide	A term used when someone is murdered
Cold case	A case that is never solved; sometimes, with new technology, it can be solved
Criminal justice	The study of the legal process of taking a case from beginning to end
DARE	Drug Abuse Resistance Education
Cadet training	The training necessary for a person to become a police officer
Patrol unit	The officers who are out on the road and who deal with situations as they arise
Detectives unit	The officers who are specifically involved with investigating any kind of crime

Lesson Objectives (with Standards Guide Words)

- Students will establish a working relationship with law enforcement individuals through an introductory visit that entails a job description and daily responsibilities along with the training involved. (Guide words: career, interview skills)

- Students will also understand concepts of the law such as individual rights and when those rights are not rights because a law is broken. Also, the rights a police officer has in juxtaposition to those of individuals, and when it becomes their duty to intervene. (Guide words: critical thinking)

- Students will be able to discern fact from opinion. (Guide words: fact, opinion)

- Students will be able to discern conclusions from generalizations. (Guide words: conclusion, generalization)

Lessons and Learning Activities

Lesson One: The Teacher as a Resource

Allotted time: thirty minutes

For students to prepare for their visitation from a law enforcement official, you should get students into the interview mode. Ask them what kind of questions would be important to ask a teacher if they were a journalist and writing a story for the newspaper. Suppose the teacher has won the teacher-of-the-year award. What kind of questions would be appropriate, and why? Write student responses on the board. Ask students what kind of questions would be inappropriate, and why. Write these on the board as well.

Then you should have one student come up in front of the room and interview the teacher using the appropriate questions. This way the correct approach to interviewing can be modeled for the entire class. After the teacher answers each question, stop and ask students to pick out the important parts of each answer. Then discuss how they should be documented. In this case, it is not necessary to write in complete sentences. Students should write short phrases or catch words that are indicative of what the person is saying. Later on, notes can be transcribed into a paragraph and edited into a story.

You can also stress the point here that there is a time and place for everything! Asking questions that are not appropriate wastes time, and if time is limited the interviewer will not get the wanted story.

Use the worksheet on page 6 to show students how to organize their interview.

Interviewing

Name of person:

Topic of interest:

Questions:

1.

2.

3.

4.

5.

Answers to questions:

1.

2.

3.

4.

5.

Summary statement completed immediately after interview:

Lesson Two: Students as Resource

Allotted time: forty minutes

Now have students pretend that they work for the local newspaper. They are in charge of interviewing students about a crime in school. Use an index card to put together an array of choices:

- A locker was spraypainted.
- A locker was broken into and money was stolen.
- A fight between two boys occurred in the cafeteria.
- Someone has written on the bathroom mirror with lipstick.

Have them interview each other to find out essential information for their article. After they have all of the answers and information, they should write a small article of approximately eight to ten sentences. The final product should contain the questions asked, the responses, and the notes taken during the interview. They should also title it and then share it with the class. You can also post them on a bulletin board.

Lesson Three: Law Enforcement Officer

Allotted time: fifty minutes

Students should now be ready to complete an interview with a law enforcement officer. Using the ideas given earlier and the worksheet, have students interview an officer.

Go through the process and have students tailor questions that are relevant and meaningful to your speaker. Remind students that there will be a follow-up discussion the next day in which they will need to bring their interview sheets. This activity takes one period to complete. You can use the handout or have students write it out on a sheet of paper.

Springboard to Writing

Allotted time: forty-five minutes

This activity is used throughout the book to generate ideas for various writing pieces. They may range from short writing pieces to three-page essays. In this springboard to writing, have students compile a small portfolio of two or three interviews. Students should discuss their "findings." They should also discuss what they learned from interviewing various subjects through pertinent facts, relevant opinions, and reasonable conclusions.

CSI Notebook

Allotted time: fifteen minutes

"CSI notebook" stands for the crime scene investigation notebook. This activity is done in the lab book at the end of a unit. It can also be handed in as homework, or a quiz grade.

Students should write a page or two about what they learned of the duties and responsibilities of law enforcement. To frame questions and suggestions, students should think about possibly pursuing a career in law enforcement. Why would they want to do it (or why not)? What are the pros? What are the cons? Could they deal with the emotional stress that comes along with the job? Students can then share answers in small groups of three or four, or as a class.

Assessment

- **Mastery (A).** After thoroughly describing the interview process, a student is able to reveal his or her finding in a clear, concise manner. Facts and opinions, and conclusions and generalizations, are clearly delineated. Language use exhibits a mature control of syntax and semantics.
- **Proficient (B).** Though this paper describes the interviewing process in some detail, the student does not write with control and clarity. He or she may have a grasp of broad concepts but has not definitively illustrated these concepts with evidence. Although a solid paper, occasional lapses reveal a lack of control.
- **Satisfactory (C).** Most papers fall into this category. The writing describes the interviewing process through anecdote. There is sparse use of detail. Broad generalizations do not exhibit a thorough understanding of relevant concepts. Syntax and semantics are satisfactory, though unsophisticated.
- **Unsatisfactory (D).** This paper does not adequately describe the interview process, objectively or anecdotally. There is poor use of detail. Syntax and semantics are unsatisfactory, unsophisticated, and there is an overall lack of quality in the prose.
- **Insufficient (F).** Insufficient papers reveal a profound lack of understanding of the interviewing process. The use of detail is very poor. Syntax and semantics are unsatisfactory and exhibit more than a casual lack of proficiency.

Lesson Accommodations and Modifications

Modifications can be made for learning support students by limiting the amount of questions asked. If a student can come up with two good questions, that is satisfactory. Also, the writing assignment can be modified to three to five sentences for the article.

If the class consists of ESL students, contact an officer who speaks Spanish (or the appropriate language) to come in for the interview.

For Further Study

If students are interested in learning more about various areas in law enforcement, or any legal field for that matter, they can read junior detective novels such as the Hardy Boys or Sherlock Holmes. Also, Court TV, Discovery, A&E, and The Learning Channel offer programs that deal with jobs in these fields. These programs should be viewed at the discretion of parents; some material is not appropriate for children. You can also record some of these programs and determine whether or not they are acceptable to show in a classroom.

References

Conklin, Barbara G., Gardner, Robert, and Shortelle, Dennis. *Encyclopedia of Forensic Science*. Phoenix: Oryx, 2002.

Douglas, John, Burgess, Anne, Burgess, Allen, and Ressler, Robert. *Crime Classification Manual*. San Francisco: Jossey-Bass, 1992.

Edwards, Martin. *Urge to Kill*. Cincinnati: Writers Digest, 2002.

Lee, Henry, and O'Neill, Thomas. *Cracking Cases: The Science of Solving Crimes*. New York: Prometheus, 2002.

Zonderman, John. *Beyond the Crime Lab*. Hoboken, N.J.: Wiley, 1999.

Chapter One

Interviewing Witnesses and Suspects

Overview for Teachers

This chapter addresses a visitation from a local detective or police officer and the litany of questions that may accompany such an interview. The chapter also broaches the subject of how to incorporate witnesses and suspects into the interviewing process. The goal in the case of a local law enforcement officer is to have him or her discuss interviewing eyewitnesses to get an account of what was observed at the crime scene. People must also be interviewed to determine whether or not they can be eliminated from the suspect list. There are important questions that must be addressed in this process. When interviewing an eyewitness, the approach differs from interviewing a suspect. The detective can explain differences between the two.

There are also certain ways the question must be worded for sensitivity. The nature of the investigation determines the types of questions used.

Questions that kids should consider asking may be similar to these:

- What is your name?
- What is your address and contact information?
- When did you arrive on the scene?
- Did you see the entire scene unfold?
- If so, can you list the events that took place in the order in which they happened?
- Do you know any of the people involved in the event?
- If so, how?
- Are you willing to come to the station to sign an affidavit?

12   *Partners in Crime*

CRIME SCENE DO NOT CROSS CRIME SCENE DO NOT CROSS CRIME SCENE DO NOT CROSS CRIME SCENE DO NOT CROSS CRIME SCENE DO NOT CROSS CRIME SCENE DO NOT CROSS CRIME SCENE

Investigating Crime Scenes in Literature

Crime scenes in literature run the full gamut of information offered to the reader. Details and events can be carefully put together to solve a crime in literature. This activity can be done with pieces of literature that are geared toward crime scenes. Any Sherlock Holmes story more than serves the purpose; there are many stories that can be applied to several chapters in this book. Encyclopedia Brown is another character in juvenile literature with several stories that can be turned into crime scenes. Finally, some of the books in the Goosebumps series may also be conducive to this treatment. If assistance is needed in developing other pieces of evidence correctly, use other chapters in this book.

Introduction to Subject Matter

(to be read to students)

Sometimes the best crime scenes and mysteries come directly from reading. Think about a book that left you hanging or turning page after page into the wee hours of the night. That is a great piece of writing. Authors pride themselves on having the ability to amaze, scare, and leave the reader in a state of confusion. Mystery and crime writers complete countless hours of research and spend time working with police detectives, investigators, and forensic scientists to enhance their knowledge about crime. Writers also need to know how to create characters who are essential to the story. They do careful planning to make their characters as lifelike as possible. Some characters are even based on actual persons; this makes the story more believable and exciting. (*Aside for the teacher:* once the students become involved in the story, you can guide them through the crime scene process by making use of witness statements, evidence, and other necessary documents.)

Vocabulary

Defense	The facts and their presentation as they relate to the defendant in a court case
Eyewitness	Somebody who sees something happen and can give evidence about it
Narrative	A story or account of a sequence of events in the order in which they happened
Prosecution	The lawyers representing the person or people who are taking legal action against somebody in a court of law, especially the state or the people in a criminal trial
Suspect	To believe that somebody may have committed a crime or wrongdoing, though without having any proof

Lesson Objectives (with Standards Guide Words)

- Students will learn the difference between eyewitness and suspect. (Guide words: definition, comparison, contrast)
- Students will identify crime scenes in literature. (Guide words: literature, reading, setting, plot, characterization)
- Students will identify eyewitnesses and suspects in literature. (Guide words: literature, reading, setting, plot, characterization)
- Students will conduct mock interviews with eyewitnesses and suspects on the basis of literature. (Guide words: interview, question, answer)
- Students will learn what the terms *defense* and *prosecution* mean and how they apply to the courtroom. (Guide words: definition, vocabulary, word study, diction)

Lesson and Learning Activity

Allotted time: three class periods; four days for final writing piece

In this case, we will look at a scene from S.E. Hinton's popular novel, *The Outsiders*. It is the scene where Bob Sheldon is stabbed by Johnny Cade. The list of evidence given here does not appear in that book; it has been made up to fit in with the crime that occurs. Also, the interview statements have been created along the lines of what people would say according to their character. Since it is a persuasive paper, the test results can be manipulated to create a guilty or not-guilty verdict. The evidence testing should be discussed in class so students know how to arrive at their conclusion. Students have the choice of taking a side: prosecution or defense. The prosecution is responsible for charging Johnny with Bob's murder, and the defense is responsible for keeping Johnny out of jail. Have students choose a side; then make an argument out of the information. This process should take one class period. The science teacher should complete this activity, since evidence and testing fits into the science curriculum.

List of Evidence from the Crime Scene

Here is a list of evidence collected from the crime scene:

- A switchblade knife was found with bloodstains on it. The blood will be tested and then fumed for fingerprints.
- Fibers and hairs were found on Bob's shirt. These will be compared to the fibers found on Johnny's body, and his own hair.
- Leaves and dirt found on Bob's body were collected for a soil analysis.
- Pictures were taken of Bob's scratched-up back. Is it from fighting, or being dragged into the bushes?

14   *Partners in Crime*

CRIME SCENE DO NOT CROSS CRIME SCENE DO NOT CROSS CRIME SCENE DO NOT CROSS CRIME SCENE DO NOT CROSS CRIME SCENE DO NOT CROSS CRIME SCENE DO NOT CROSS CRIME SCENE

- Fingernail scrapings were taken from Johnny. These will be tested to see if Bob's DNA shows up. This will also indicate if the scratches on Bob came from his struggle, or when Johnny dragged Bob's body into the bushes.

- A flask was found, smelling of whiskey.

- A hospital report on Johnny was filed. Pictures were taken of the bruises on his face. Do the bruises match Bob's rings? What are the colors of the bruises? Are they old or new?

- A water sample was taken from Johnny's lungs. Do the microbes in his lungs match the microbes found in the fountain at the park?

After looking at the evidence collected, review the witness statements taken at the police station. Two boys were picked up walking along the street. One was wearing a sweatshirt and jeans that were drenched; the other was wearing a denim jacket and jeans. The boy with the jacket had red stains on his hands, the right jacket sleeve, and the right cuff of his jeans.

The names of the two boys were Johnny Cade and Ponyboy Curtis; both were known as "greasers." The boys were hauled in to the station and questioned. Ponyboy Curtis gave his statement first. The next person brought in for questioning was Randy Adderson. Police picked him up at the phone booth where he called 911. At the hospital, Bob Sheldon was pronounced DOA (dead on arrival). Randy was present during the entire event when Bob was stabbed. The detective placed him alone in the room to get his side of the story. Randy was very shaken up and scared. He was terribly upset about the loss of Bob. His account of what happened is given here.

After reading both statements, draw a T-chart on the board to determine differences in the two stories. Then discuss how people perceive events differently when they are on one side or another.

Eyewitness Statement from Ponyboy Curtis

Johnny and I were out in the lot and we fell asleep. When I woke up, I didn't know what time it was, so I went home. When I got home, my brother Darry yelled at me and hit me in the face. I was real mad, so I ran out of the house to find Johnny. We was planning on runnin' away. After I found him, we went to the park so I could blow off some steam. I was downright mad and about to punch something. Johnny and I had a smoke on the monkey bars and a blue Mustang came up to us. A couple of Socs [the Socials] got out of the car. I could tell they were drunk because they were swayin' and slurrin' their speech. I told Johnny to stay put and we could handle them. I told Johnny to get his blade ready if we needed it. They approached us and Bob said, "Do you know what a Greaser is?" Then he said, "White trash with long greasy hair."

Then Bob threw liquor on me from his flask. It smelled like whiskey. Then I said, "Do you know what a Soc is?" Bob gazed at me with a drunk

Interviewing Witnesses and Suspects

15

CRIME SCENE DO NOT CROSS CRIME SCENE DO NOT CROSS CRIME SCENE DO NOT CROSS CRIME SCENE DO NOT CROSS CRIME SCENE DO NOT CROSS CRIME SCENE DO NOT CROSS CRIME SCENE

stare. I said, "White trash with Mustangs and Madras shirts." Then I spit a goober in his eye and started to run. They chased us down and three of them tried to drown me in the fountain. The boys were Bob, Randy, and Brad.

They kept dunkin' me until I thought I was gonna die. Then everything went blurry and I woke up next to a dead guy. It was Bob. I found Johnny sittin' up against the fountain crying. Johnny said that Bob was trying to drown him too, so he took out his blade and jammed it into Bob's stomach. As I regained my focus, Johnny explained that he had to do it to save our lives. He fought off Bob and scratched him up pretty good on his back. I was scared and wanted to get outa there. We dragged the body into the bushes and started walking away from the park. That's when you picked us up.

Eyewitness Statement from Randy Adderson

We were out drinking, which I know we aren't supposed to do. Bob was really drunk, and we wanted him to sober up before we took him home. He looked out the window and saw two boys sitting in the park smoking cigarettes. Bob started going crazy when he recognized them as the boys who tried to pick up his girlfriend. We thought it might be good for him to blow off some steam, so we went to the park and got out of the car. We then walked towards the boys and asked them what they were doing there. They said, "This is our turf. Get lost, you stinky dirtbags." Then the boy in the denim jacket spit in Bob's face. They turned around and began running. One of them fell in the fountain when he tripped and rolled in the water. We pulled him out of the water and restrained him. He was kicking and screaming at us, saying he was going to kill us. We laughed at him because there was four of us and two them. We didn't touch the boys. We didn't have a chance. Right after we pinned down the boy that fell in the water, the other came running out of the bushes and stabbed Bob in the stomach. Blood was dripping everywhere. We all ran because we didn't want to get hurt. We figured that Bob was dead. Then we went to the diner to figure out our stories, so nobody could place us with Bob at the time of the murder. Then we decided that we should tell the cops about Bob's body. That's when we made the call from the phone on the corner. I guess you traced it and the cops came and picked us up. Here we are.

Johnny agreed that his story was exactly the same as Ponyboy described it. The detective then asked Johnny if he could have some fingernail clippings to see if Bob's DNA showed up to prove there was a struggle. They also took fiber samples from Johnny's jacket and hair for fiber testing. They also extracted some blood to identify the type and DNA. Johnny was then printed and photographed by the detective.

Now, have students look at the questions presented here. They should write out their answers to each question. This will help them acquire necessary information for their paper.

Questions to Consider

1. Why would Johnny use his knife to defend himself and his friend?
2. What characteristics about Johnny display his potential to be dangerous?
3. What characteristics about Bob led him to his death?
4. What characteristics about Johnny's childhood and family background reveal his reaction to the scene at the park?
5. Why does Bob wear such large rings on his fingers?
6. What personality traits about Bob explain his behavior?

Questions of this kind can be applied to any character in any piece of literature. Other questions can be developed too that are relevant to investigating characters or criminals. Using these questions also teaches students methods of inquiry, analysis, and hypothesizing.

Now that students have the evidence, try to piece together this crime scene in the courtroom. Make judgments that are based on a combination of the evidence provided. Also focus on the differences in the stories of the eyewitnesses. How can we tell if one is lying or not? Good luck, and may the better attorney win!

Although students do not know the correct procedure for collecting and testing all of this evidence, have them write what they think would be the correct way to do so. Students will learn the correct procedures and processes later on. For now, see if they can hypothesize about the process of collecting and testing evidence.

This is also a perfect time to have a lawyer come in to speak to students about prosecuting or defending a case. If a county courthouse is nearby, a local attorney may be a terrific source of information, especially for juvenile cases. You should have him or her come in to speak about what the job is of each side in the trial. He or she should also know about rules that have to be followed, and the judicial process. This might help students decide if they want to be the prosecution or the defense. Most lawyers have a book that is filled with penal codes for juveniles that they use every day. They can share them with the class, along with questions that students generate using the guidelines in the introduction. This activity can be done by combining both English and science classes. It should take one class period.

Springboard to Writing

Allotted time: thirty minutes
After students have finished, have them reflect on the choices they made in their paper. Why did they choose to prosecute or defend Johnny Cade? Ask them to cite examples that might have shaped their believing one story or the other. The writing piece should be one page in length, single-spaced.

Interviewing Witnesses and Suspects　　　　　　　　　　　**17**

CRIME SCENE DO NOT CROSS CRIME SCENE DO NOT CROSS CRIME SCENE DO NOT CROSS CRIME SCENE DO NOT CROSS CRIME SCENE DO NOT CROSS CRIME SCENE DO NOT CROSS CRIME SCENE

CSI Notebook

Allotted time: fifteen minutes

Show students a short video clip from a movie scene. Choose a busy scene in which a crime occurs. The clip should not be longer than thirty seconds. Have students write down everything they saw. Then generate a list on the board, and have students keep track of how many items they remembered. Also have them pick out distractions that make it difficult to remember everything. What did they focus on the most? You will get varied responses and explanations.

Assessment

Assess the completed writing piece using this rubric:

- **Mastery (A).** Student uses all pieces of evidence and clearly explains the function of the evidence in the case. Witness statements are thoroughly read and used correctly in conjunction with the evidence. Student displays a succinct order of events and organization.
- **Proficient (B).** Student uses most of the evidence presented and ties it in with the witness statements. Student has an adequate order of events and organization.
- **Satisfactory (C).** Student uses only the evidence portion or only the eyewitness accounts to make the argument. There is no apparent consistency in the order of events or organization.
- **Unsatisfactory (D).** Student uses minimal evidence and witness accounts. Student does not choose a side. No order of events or organization.
- **Insufficient (F).** Student does not use any evidence or witness accounts. Paper rambles and does not make a point about the case.

Lesson Accommodations and Modifications

For learning support students, use graphic organizers to sort out evidence. Students can first decide which side they will choose. Then the organizer can be set up to present the evidence and how it proves their side. A T-chart can also be used as a graphic organizer to help sort out the eyewitness accounts.

For Further Study

Any student interested in pursuing a degree in law can prepare a five-minute presentation. In the presentation, he or she can explain one area of law that is appealing. Duties, responsibilities, training, and schooling should be the focus of the presentation.

18   *Partners in Crime*

CRIME SCENE DO NOT CROSS CRIME SCENE DO NOT CROSS CRIME SCENE DO NOT CROSS CRIME SCENE DO NOT CROSS CRIME SCENE DO NOT CROSS CRIME SCENE DO NOT CROSS CRIME SCENE

To become a police officer or detective, a person must be at least nineteen years of age or older and possess a high school diploma or GED equivalent. Another requirement might be college hours in a criminal justice program. The person should also have a driver's license and the physical strength and agility to perform the duties of a police officer.

A written and oral examination is involved, in which the person must score 70 percent or higher. He or she must also pass a physical test. A medical and psychological examination is performed, along with a background investigation check.

The job description of a detective is one who uses various techniques, such as interviews, searches, surveillance, and background checks to gather evidence and verify facts about an incident or person.

To become eligible for this position, a person must make it through a probationary period ranging from six months to three years. Once appointed to the position, the applicant must be interviewed by senior officers. They look for personal characteristics such as honesty, integrity, and a sense of responsibility. The officer must pass written and oral examinations as well as hearing, vision, agility, and strength testing. If the officer passes all of these exams, he or she will complete a recruit training program for twelve to fourteen weeks.

References

Roberts, Gillian. *You Can Write a Mystery.* Cincinnati: Writers Digest Books, 1999.

Treat, Lawrence. *Crime and Puzzlement, vol. 3.* Boston: David Godine, 1999.

Chapter Two

Crime Scene Procedure

Overview for Teachers

Crime scene integrity is crucial to any investigation. Police receive thorough training on how to appropriately collect evidence so nothing is compromised. This is also one of the jobs of the defense lawyer, to make sure the police do their job correctly. Failing to do a task as simple as signing a name on a piece of evidence tape can keep it from being admitted into court. Also, there are strict guidelines as to who may enter the crime scene; a protocol is rigidly followed. There are many people involved in investigating a crime, and all of them play their respective roles at different times in the investigation.

It starts with the responding officer, the first person at the scene. It is his or her job to assess if an ambulance or the fire department is needed, or more backup (including the detectives unit). The responding officer can also be responsible for trying to save a victim's life until the paramedics arrive.

If the situation requires the detectives unit to respond, a chain of custody must be established. Specific steps are adhered to when detectives and other officials arrive at a crime scene. These people range from the paramedics, firefighters, and fire police (in some states, such as Pennsylvania) to the county coroner.

The job of the paramedics is to attempt to save the lives of the injured at the scene. In some instances, the paramedics have to place tubes or other apparatus to try to keep the injured person alive. This must be documented, because crucial evidence can be compromised or lost.

The job of the firefighters and fire police is to take care of any fire-related problems that arise. The fire police are used to direct traffic around the scene and give detour directions for drivers who do not know their way.

Depending on the county, a coroner may come to the scene of the crime to pronounce the person dead. Then he or she takes the body to a hospital morgue, where an autopsy is performed. If there is an ME (medical examiner), the body is delivered to the office of the medical examiner for an autopsy. The medical examiner is a forensic pathologist who specializes in autopsies where legal implications are involved.

20   *Partners in Crime*

CRIME SCENE DO NOT CROSS CRIME SCENE DO NOT CROSS CRIME SCENE DO NOT CROSS CRIME SCENE DO NOT CROSS CRIME SCENE DO NOT CROSS CRIME SCENE DO NOT CROSS CRIME SCENE

Once the crime scene is cleared, the detectives stay behind to interview witnesses or speak to other officials and compare notes. This can help an investigation by bringing other areas of expertise to the case.

Now that a rapport has been developed with the local authorities, arrange a time for a lecture on crime scene integrity and establishing a chain of custody. Suggest they explain the importance of evidence contamination and properly tagging the evidence. They should bring along all of the materials needed to properly secure a crime scene area. You can also have them discuss what multiple crime scene areas are and how to follow a progression if any is evident.

Before anyone goes near the crime scene, it must first be secured with police tape. It should cover more than the immediate crime scene, because other evidence could be around in the area. The detectives make the decision of how far the secure area extends.

Next, a crime scene entry log must be created. (See page 21.) It contains the name of every person who enters the crime scene. This item is requested in court to ensure that the only people at the crime scene are those essential to the investigation. In some cases, only specified police officers are allowed to enter the crime scene. If too many people are involved, evidence can be compromised and the perpetrator could walk free.

Crime Scene Entry Log

Location: _____

_____

Present on scene (officer in charge, police, EMS, coroner) _____

_____

_____

_____

_____

_____

_____

Date and time established: _____

Officer maintaining log (name and signature): _____

_____

Incident no.: _____

22   *Partners in Crime*

CRIME SCENE DO NOT CROSS CRIME SCENE DO NOT CROSS CRIME SCENE DO NOT CROSS CRIME SCENE DO NOT CROSS CRIME SCENE DO NOT CROSS CRIME SCENE DO NOT CROSS CRIME SCENE

The next step is to establish a chain of custody. This basically means that there should be witnesses present to verify that all of the evidence tagged is the same as what is eventually presented in a court of law. The chain of custody establishes four things:

1. Who is directly in contact with evidence
2. Verification of the date and time the evidence was collected
3. The circumstances under which the evidence was handled
4. Any changes that have been made to the evidence during the collection

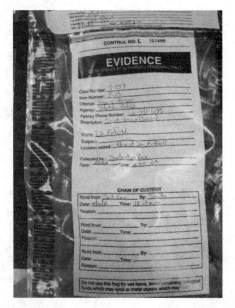

Once the chain of custody has been established, the detective or technician begins the process of tagging all evidence. This is imperative so that evidence can be identified later on in the investigation. It also provides solid credibility to the jury in a courtroom.

All evidence at the crime should be tagged. The label of each bag should have certain information:

- Description of the item
- Police case number and identifier
- Date
- Location of the evidence
- Name of the person who collected the evidence
- Any serial number or identifying garment information

If you ask, the detectives may donate some evidence bags for use in the classroom. They will also give you some crime scene tape to be used during an activity.

Filling out a Crime Scene Checklist

Processing a crime scene is not as easy as it looks. Officers need to be able to write effectively to fill out forms and document their findings. Just as teachers expect students to spend a lot of time drafting and revising, officers must spend time taking notes and making sure they understand them well enough to file a report back at the office.

No detail can be left out. Every inch of the crime scene must be investigated. There are a couple of forms that may be used depending on the crime involved, whether a car accident, death scene, or robbery site. See the sample homicide report beginning on page 23.

Homicide Report

Name of deceased: _____
                             First   Middle   Last

Address: _____

_____

Age: _____ Race: _____

Sex: M F Telephone number: _____

Marital status: S M W D Separated Unknown

Next of kin:

Name: _____

Address: _____

Telephone number: _____

Police notified by: _____ Police arrived at scene: _____

Date: _____ Time: _____ Date: _____ Time: _____

Name: _____ Address: _____

_____ Weather conditions: _____

Telephone number: _____

Relationship to deceased: _____

Deceased found:

Date: _____ Time: _____

Location: Apartment House Townhouse Other (describe): _____

Entrance: Key Cutting chain Forcing door Other (describe): _____

Type of lock on door: _____

Condition of other doors and windows: Open Closed Locked Unlocked

Body found:

Living room   Dining room   Bedroom   Kitchen   Attic   Basement
Other (describe): _____

Location in the room: _____

Position of the body: On face   On back   Other _____

Condition of body: _____

Fully clothed   Partially clothed   Unclothed

Preservation: Well preserved   Decomposed

Estimated rigor: Complete   Head   Arms   Legs

Livor [see text]:   Front   Back   Localized

Color: _____

Blood: Absent   Present   Location: _____

Ligatures: Yes   No

Apparent wounds: None   Gunshot   Stab   Blunt force

Number: _____

Location: Head   Neck   Chest   Abdomen   Extremities

Hanging: Yes   No   Means _____

Weapons present:

Gun (estimated caliber) _____

Type: _____

Knife: _____

Other (describe): _____

Condition of surroundings: Orderly   Untidy   Disarray

Odors: Decomposition   Other: _____

Evidence of last food preparation: _____

Where: _____

Type: _____

Dated material:

Mail: _____

Newspaper: _____

TV Guide: _____

Last contact with the deceased:

Date: _____

Type of contact: _____

Name of contact: _____

Evidence of robbery: Yes   No   Not determined

Identification of deceased: Yes   No

If yes, how accomplished? _____

If no, how is it to be accomplished? _____

Evidence of drug use (prescription or nonprescription):   Yes   No

(If drugs present, collect them and send with the body)

Evidence of drug paraphernalia: Yes   No

Type: _____

Narrative:

_____

_____

_____

_____

_____

When describing the crime scene, there is some important information for the teacher to understand.

Lividity is the color of the body. Technically, it is called *livor mortis*. It is a Latin term that means "color of death." In the beginning stages of death, a process called autolysis occurs. This is the breakdown of blood cells within the body. As they decompose, the ruptured blood cells settle in parts of the body where the gravitational pull is strongest. As they settle, they begin to stain those areas. A normal lividity color is a reddish-purplish hue. In instances of poisoning through carbon monoxide, chemicals, or drugs, the color can turn bright red.

Lividity changes as the process of decomposition continues. It can range from purple to red, green, or black. After approximately two to four hours, depending on weather conditions, lividity sets into the area where it has settled. If the body is moved from its original position, the stains remain. If the body is moved before it is set, the process starts over, but the original stains are still present. This helps investigators determine if the body has been moved within the first couple of hours after death.

In the case of an object resting under the body where the blood settles, sometimes it turns white because the skin is raised above the area where gravity is strongest. This is called "blanching." After the lividity sets, the blanched areas stay permanent until further decomposition occurs.

Rigor mortis is the process that occurs after death. The Latin phrase means "stiff." Temperature plays a major role in the time it takes for the body to go through the full process of rigor. Within one to three hours, rigor begins, usually in the jaw area. It involves formation of linking chemical bridges between actin and myosin. It does not shorten the muscles. Full rigor is established when the jaw, elbow, and knee joints are frozen. Rigor mortis can be broken if the joints are moved; this is sometimes difficult because the more muscle mass the harder it is to break the rigor.

After approximately twenty-four to thirty-six hours, rigor mortis reverses and the body becomes limp. Although rigor begins in the jaw, it does not work its way down the body. It happens in the smaller joints first and progresses to the larger ones.

In some instances, there is such a thing as instantaneous rigor. This is called a "cadaveric spasm." It is sometimes seen in the case of a drowning or fire victim. This happens when all muscles tighten up at once, causing the body to become stiff. The victim's hands are usually in a fist shape and held out to their sides, as though the person is preparing to do a bench press.

Algor mortis is the temperature of the body. It is Latin meaning "chill of death." On average, the body cools anywhere from 1.5 to 2 degrees an hour, highly dependent on the ambient air temperature. The temperature is usually taken in one of two ways. The liver is a great organ to get an accurate reading; if it is too badly damaged, the temperature should be taken in the rectum. Depending on the circumstances, the temperature can be taken at the scene of the crime, or if that is not feasible then at the morgue.

Ligatures are marks that are left on the body, showing some kind of restraint. When they appear on the neck, it is usually due to strangulation or asphyxiation.

Sometimes marks left on the neck match with evidence found at the crime scene. For example, suppose an extension cord is used to strangle the victim. If the cord is

Crime Scene Procedure

27

CRIME SCENE DO NOT CROSS CRIME SCENE DO NOT CROSS CRIME SCENE DO NOT CROSS CRIME SCENE DO NOT CROSS CRIME SCENE DO NOT CROSS CRIME SCENE DO NOT CROSS CRIME SCENE

left at the crime scene, it will match the bruises on the neck. In the case of manual strangulation, bruising occurs, and during the autopsy hemorrhaging is evident underneath the surface in the dermis area. Another strong indicator of manual strangulation is a broken hyoid bone. The hyoid is a U-shaped bone at the base of the tongue.

When wounds on the body are encountered, they must be looked at closely to identify the type of injury. Gunshots at close range leave residue on the clothing, as well as an entrance wound. This powder can be collected and sent to the lab for analysis.

Wounds from a knife usually have a clean cut that separates the layers of skin and muscle. The angle and penetration of the wound can also tell you the position in which the victim was attacked.

Blunt force trauma usually leaves messy, open wounds on the surface. During autopsy, hemorrhaging is seen underneath the wound. Also, an X ray should be taken to establish internal damage to the skeleton.

Evidence of last food preparation may be found at the crime scene. It is also discovered at the autopsy when the gastric contents are emptied from the stomach and sent to the lab for analysis.

If any of these conditions are observed at the crime scene, pictures must be taken and documented. Photographs should be taken at various angles and ranges to ensure complete documentation.

Collecting Evidence: DNA

There is a prescribed protocol that must be followed when collecting DNA evidence. Any investigating officer will tell you that it is a must to follow the rules at all times. These are some of the rules they have to follow.

Upon arrival, information from the first responding officer should be collected. Find out when he or she arrived and what is known so far. Next, points of entrance and exit should be established; these are the only points that should be used to enter or exit the crime scene. An officer should be appointed to be in charge of the crime scene log to monitor all people entering and exiting the crime scene. As investigators walk through the crime scene, they should identify possible sources of DNA. Everything should be documented, with photos, video, and diagrams if necessary. The more precise the information, the easier things are for the investigators.

When a blood source is identified, it should be noted whether it is wet or dry when discovered. This gives some approximation of time as to how long it has been there. Obviously, if it has dried completely it will be difficult to establish how long it has been there. Blood dries from the outside in, becoming crusty and eventually changing to a dark reddish brown color.

If bloodstain patterns are present, document them with photos and list reference points before they are collected. Bloodstain patterns are discussed later in this chapter.

When handling blood, it is imperative that all safety precautions be taken. Blood can contain sexually transmitted diseases, hepatitis, or HIV. A person cannot catch a disease by merely touching the blood; there has to be some sort of opening in the skin for the contaminated substance to get into the body. Even the most minute of cuts is susceptible, which is why gloves are necessary all the time.

The person responsible for collecting the evidence should determine the need for protective equipment. He or she should also secure a location for disposal of biohazardous materials such as used gloves and instruments.

The technicians who collect this kind of evidence should wear latex gloves. It is highly recommended that they wear double sets of gloves, so when they change gloves to collect the next specimen they are still covered so as not to contaminate the evidence. Sometimes when technicians change gloves, skin cells fall from their hands and contaminate the evidence; doubling up helps keep the integrity of the evidence. The technicians should also wear shoe covers, protective eyewear, and sometimes even gowns.

The first thing that should be collected is evidence that is considered to be fragile. Environmental factors such as light and precipitation should weigh heavily on the time allowed to collect the evidence. If the blood sample is left in the light too long, the environment could degrade it, while precipitation could wash it away totally. This is one reason why victims are often thrown into waterways—it washes a lot of the evidence away.

Procedures for collection of blood evidence are very clear cut and expected to be followed at all times. All pieces of evidence are always collected and packed separately. Each one should be labeled with the name of the technician, date, time, ID number, where it was found, and how it was collected.

Articles of clothing should never be folded over on themselves. If two separate blood sources touch each other, it could contaminate the entire sample. Use a piece of paper to separate them; it should be folded so it protects the stained areas of the garment.

Clothing containing blood evidence is collected in paper bags. Storing it in plastic can cause bacteria to grow and degrade or ruin the evidence. Therefore, a plastic bag should only be used if an item is soaked with blood and needs to be removed. In this case, it should be taken to a secure area and handled properly.

When collecting the sample, if possible submit the entire item. There have been cases where crime scene technicians have used saws to cut out walls to submit as evidence. A door can be taken off its hinges; car seats have been removed and submitted altogether.

When collecting blood evidence that is wet, these are the steps that should be followed. If at all possible, submit the entire item. If this is not an option, use a cotton swab. It is best to use single-sided swabs. Since the stain is wet, it is not necessary to moisten the end with distilled water. After the sample is swabbed, it should be documented where it was found and how wet it was. Then let the swab air dry before packaging. Every swab that is taken should be placed in a separate container and immediately stored in a refrigerated area.

In the case of a small stain, try to concentrate the blood on the tip of the swab. This will make it easier to extract the DNA at the laboratory.

When a dry bloodstain is encountered, different steps are taken. Of course, if the entire sample can be submitted, then that is best. If not, use a clean, fresh razor blade or scalpel to cut out the stain. Label it and package it as described here. A control sample must also be cut out to test; this should be done with a new blade or scalpel.

If the blood is on a surface that cannot be cut, use a clean, fresh razor blade, scalpel, or index card; scrape the sample onto a white piece of paper and fold it as a pharmacist would. (Do not use tape lifter to recover blood samples.) The folded paper should then be placed in an envelope and labeled appropriately. Adjacent areas should be swabbed too for a control.

Crime Scene Procedure

29

CRIME SCENE DO NOT CROSS CRIME SCENE DO NOT CROSS CRIME SCENE DO NOT CROSS CRIME SCENE DO NOT CROSS CRIME SCENE DO NOT CROSS CRIME SCENE DO NOT CROSS CRIME SCENE DO NOT CROSS CRIME SCENE

Sometimes a smear is available for blood evidence collection. In that case, use a swab and moisten it with some distilled water. Work the swab to concentrate the sample to the tip of the swab. Let it air dry and follow the correct labeling procedures. Always make sure the evidence is stored at the correct temperature to prevent degradation of the sample.

Semen and saliva are also great sources of DNA. In the case of rape and sexual assault, semen and saliva can be collected in several forms. A rape kit is a common instrument used to collect evidence at hospitals around the world. Saliva can be collected from spit left on clothing, around a bite mark, or elsewhere on the victim's body.

Tissues are also valuable in collecting DNA evidence. They should be dried, collected, and labeled appropriately.

Although spitting is a nasty habit, it has convicted criminals in the past. If a perpetrator spits on the ground, it becomes "public property," which can be collected by a detective and submitted to a lab. Soda cans, gum, and cigarette butts are also a great way to acquire DNA evidence without having to get a search warrant.

Sometimes when there is a struggle the victim fights back and gets some of the perpetrator's skin cells underneath the fingernails. Fingernails can be scraped with a round-edged toothpick and placed on a piece of paper. It should then be folded in pharmacist style and labeled appropriately. If more than one nail is scraped, a new toothpick should be used to prevent contamination.

All evidence should be sealed with evidence tape and signed by the technician who collected it, to ensure that no one else has touched that piece of evidence. It should also be properly stored to keep it from degrading.

Collecting Evidence: Fingerprints

Dusting for fingerprints should be the last step completed at a crime scene. All other evidence should be collected and secured before dusting for prints. The dust is very messy and sticks to everything. Also, if you try to wipe it off, it just smears (though it does come off easily with soap and water).

Lifting prints can be done in several ways. First, it depends on the type of surface, which falls into two categories: porous and nonporous. The first thing that should be done is to look for any visible prints. If none are found, black powder is usually applied to reveal any prints. If prints are found, they should automatically be photographed and documented. Use a one-to-one lens (where the picture is the actual size of the print) to get the true shape and size of the print. This is also necessary for it to be processed through AFIS (Automated Fingerprint Identification System).

In the case of a dark surface where black powder does not help, white powder or fluorescent powder may be applied. Fluorescent powders are great because students can use an alternative light source to show up the print. Lasers used to be the norm, but they have since been replaced by ultraviolet and other light sources. If you do use a light source, the best is a UV black light. Regular black lights work, but the UV ones are better.

Ninhydrin is another method for developing prints. It is best used on paper. It causes a reaction with the amino acids in sweat and creates a purple color. This reaction can also be produced by reacting with proteins and polypeptides. Therefore other

30   *Partners in Crime*

CRIME SCENE DO NOT CROSS CRIME SCENE DO NOT CROSS CRIME SCENE DO NOT CROSS CRIME SCENE DO NOT CROSS CRIME SCENE DO NOT CROSS CRIME SCENE DO NOT CROSS CRIME SCENE

bodily fluids that react with Ninhydrin are blood, saliva, semen, and urine. These prints should immediately be photographed. If left, they fade away as time elapses. Also, use Ninhydrin in a well-ventilated area. The fumes can cause some people to cough and hold their nose. It stinks but is a good way to show a chemical reaction.

In instances where powders might not be the best choice, superglue fuming can be used. The technical term is cyanoacrylate fuming. Basically, superglue contains methyl or ethyl cyanoacrylate ester as the active ingredient. This reacts with amino acids, fatty acids, and proteins. In the presence of moisture, a polymer is formed; when it becomes visible to the naked eye, it is white. Cyanowands can be purchased from crime scene companies, or you can create them on your own. Purchase a ten-gallon fish tank, place the item to be fumed inside the tank, fill a cup with hot water, and place a lamp inside with a seventy-five-watt bulb. Lastly, cut a soda can in half and place three or four drops of super glue in there. Seal the tank and place it in a ventilated area. Then students can watch as the reaction takes place and turns any fingerprints that have been left on the object white. The only drawback to the fish tank is that the glass will eventually become white too, and it does not wash off.

Fuming is used on garbage bags, with any kind of tape, guns, knives, the inside of an automobile, or any other surface that is smooth and nonporous.

If there is no detective in the area who can give students the necessary materials, you can purchase products from a crime scene company—or use crushed charcoal. For lifting tape, students can use packaging tape to lift prints.

If your budget does allow purchasing materials, buy different color powders, magnetic ones, and so on. Conduct an experiment using these powders and find out how they reveal or do not reveal prints. Students should note the definition in each print.

Collecting Evidence: Fibers

The detective or technician identifies fibers at the crime scene. An alternative light source may also be used to identify hairs and fibers not easily seen by the naked eye. If collecting hairs, package them in paper since there may be DNA available; packaging in plastic can promote bacteria growth and degrade the sample. When collecting hairs and fibers, follow these guidelines:

Crime Scene Procedure

31

CRIME SCENE DO NOT CROSS CRIME SCENE DO NOT CROSS CRIME SCENE DO NOT CROSS CRIME SCENE DO NOT CROSS CRIME SCENE DO NOT CROSS CRIME SCENE DO NOT CROSS CRIME SCENE

- If possible, collect the entire item. If that is not possible, use a pair of clean and sterile tweezers to pick up the item and carefully place it in the appropriate package. Make sure the item is not kinked, folded, or crushed in the process.
- If an evidence sweeper is used, remove the accumulated material in the filter bag and place it in an evidence bag. Do not use regular envelopes because small particles can escape.
- Make sure the correct documentation is on the evidence bag or container.
- If available, also collect a control sample to submit to the lab.

Collecting Evidence: Firearms, Bullets, and Gunshot Residue

If a weapon is found at the crime scene, contact a qualified crime scene technician. The investigator should assume that the gun is loaded and not touch it. Some investigators have been trained how to handle firearms and related evidence. Gunshot residue and spent bullets can also be collected by a certified technician or detective. To collect gunshot residue, follow these steps:

- Put on latex gloves.
- Using a cotton swab in a dilution of 5 percent nitric acid, swab the suspected area thoroughly.
- Place the swab in an evidence container and fill out the appropriate documentation.
- Take a control sample by using another swab in the same dilution, and place it in an evidence container labeled "control swab."

If a spent casing is found at a crime scene, the inside of the casing may be swabbed using distilled water and packaged and labeled appropriately. If a spent casing is to be collected, (1) remove the casing from the object with a clean tool, leaving the surrounding material on the casing; and (2) wrap each bullet separately in cotton, place it in a separate container, and label it appropriately.

It is important to make sure that the casing is not scratched in any way, shape, or form. This could change the outcome of the firearm identification.

Procedures for Investigating

After detectives are finished at the crime scene, they begin the search for a suspect and any clues that might lead to an arrest. Many interviews are conducted; detectives must document everything that is said. A witness statement form (see page 33) or affidavit can be filled out. The latter is a sworn statement in writing or a declaration signed and made upon an oath before an authorized magistrate.

32

Partners in Crime

CRIME SCENE DO NOT CROSS CRIME SCENE DO NOT CROSS CRIME SCENE DO NOT CROSS CRIME SCENE DO NOT CROSS CRIME SCENE DO NOT CROSS CRIME SCENE DO NOT CROSS CRIME SCENE

If the detectives think they have probable cause to search a suspect's personal property, a search and seizure warrant is required. The suspect can sign a consent form that waives his or her rights or go to the station and wait for an attorney and the correct warrant. If they do choose to fill out the consent form, it may look something like the one shown on page 34.

When police are ready to make an arrest, they obtain an arrest warrant from the judge. Once the suspect is located, the person is read his or her Miranda rights. If this is not done, a case can be thrown out of court. What it does is tell a person that he or she does not have to say anything without an attorney present. It also says that the person may answer any question that is asked and can stop at any time he or she wishes. A form used for this purpose is on page 35. Another good idea is to have a video of the signing by the officer and the person being arrested.

Some departments use a checklist for misdemeanors and felony arrests. (See page 36.) This is another valuable document to have in the courtroom. A defense lawyer sometimes looks for a way to get the client off on a technicality. The lawyer would also like to make sure that the police and other people involved in the investigation follow the law. It is the job of every person involved in the investigation to tell the truth and follow the prescribed rules for investigation.

If there is a burglary, a form is used to document all of the items stolen, along with a description in case an item is found. It also documents what the detective did to find any physical evidence of a suspect. The form looks like the one beginning on page 37.

Statement Form

Name: _____ DOB/age: _____ Case number: _____

Address: _____

_____

Telephone: _____ Date: _____

Place of interview: _____

Beginning time: _____ Ending time: _____

Officer: _____ Signature: _____

Statement: _____

_____

_____

_____

_____

_____

_____

_____

_____

_____

_____

_____

_____

_____

_____

_____

Signature: _____ Date: _____ Time: _____

Search and Seizure Consent Form

I, _____, have been informed of my consti-
tutional rights to not have a search of the location listed on this paper.
The only way a search can be made at this time is if a search warrant is
legally issued by a judge. Although aware of my right to not allow the
search to be performed, I hereby authorize _____ and
other officers to conduct a full-scale search of _____.
I have been made aware that the police are looking for evidence that
may be of value in this (these) crime(s), such as _____

_____

_____.

     I am also authorizing the officer to seize what deems appropriate. I
also realize that any evidence taken can and will be used in a court of
law. Therefore, I hereby authorize the abovesaid officer to conduct the
search without my speaking to an attorney beforehand.

Witness signature: _____ Date: _____

Name and address: _____

_____

_____

Case number: _____

The Reading of Miranda Rights and Waiver of Attorney

Time: _____

Date: _____

Location: _____

Reason for arrest: _____

Officer who is reading the rights and waiver: _____

Miranda Rights

You have the right to remain silent. Anything you say can and will be used against you in a court of law. You also have the right to talk to an attorney before questioning and to have an attorney present with you during questioning. If you cannot afford to hire an attorney, one will be appointed to represent you without charge before any questioning, if you so desire. If you decide to answer questions, you may stop any time you wish and you cannot be forced to continue.

Waiver of having an attorney present:

I fully understand the statement warning me of my rights and I am willing to answer questions. I do not want an attorney and understand that I may stop answering questions anytime during questioning. No promises have been made to me, nor have I been threatened in any manner.

Signature: _____

Date: _____

Witness(es): _____

_____

Signature of arresting officer: _____

Misdemeanor or Felony Arrest Checklist

Defendant: _____ Arrest number: _____

Officer: _____ Date: _____ Time: _____

Charges: _____

___ Defendant has been read Miranda rights with the form attached to the file. The defendant has also signed or initialed the card.

___ The name of the defendant has been run through NCIC (National Crime Information Center) and CLEAN (Commonwealth Law Enforcement Assistance Network, in Pennsylvania). Criminal history has been checked and request for a rap (record of arrests and prosecutions) sheet has been made.

___ Defendant has provided a voluntary statement. Defendant has also signed each page of the document.

___ Criminal complaint, affidavit, and arrest reports have been completed and signed by the officer.

Processing

___ Personal history sheet of defendant has been completed.

___ Defendant has been photographed.

___ Defendant has been fingerprinted for federal and state records.

___ If defendant has not been processed, please explain why not here:

_____

_____

Evidence

___ Property Evidence Record Form has been completed. It has also been placed in the evidence room.

___ An entry has been logged into the Property/Evidence book. The number is: _____.

DUI Arrest

___ DUI arrest folder has been completed.

___ Chemical testing form has been completed.

___ The form and sample are together in proper storage (refrigerator).

___ DUI arrest report has been completed.

Burglary Investigation Form

Name of victim: _____

Date of report: _____

Address: _____

_____

Home phone: _____ Work phone: _____

Case number: _____

<u>Checklist of Evidence Search</u>

Was there any physical evidence?   Yes   No

Were fingerprints available, and if so, were any lifted?   Yes   No

What is the location of the fingerprint(s)?

_____

Are there any signs of forced entry or pry marks?   Yes   No

Were impressions of the marks made?   Yes   No

Was any other physical evidence found at the scene?   Yes   No

If yes, list the evidence here: _____

Were photos taken?   Yes   No   If yes, what was photographed?

_____

<u>List of property taken:</u> Have victim make a list on a separate sheet of paper. If person does not have one ready, it can be submitted within the next two days. Also have person list the name, make, model, and any model or serial numbers. Person should also list the approximate value of each item.

<u>Contact names</u>

Person one: name and address   Person two: name and address

_____   _____

_____   _____

_____   _____

Person three: name and address   Person four: name and address

_____   _____

_____   _____

_____   _____

Have there been any other burglaries in the area?   Yes   No

If so, when and where? _____

Has anyone worked on the house recently?   Yes   No

If so, when and what kind of work? _____

Have any deliveries been made recently?   Yes   No

If so, when? _____

What rooms were entered? _____

Were any parts of the house ransacked?   Yes   No

If so, which ones? _____

Is there any evidence of food, drinks, or tobacco use throughout the house?   Yes   No

If so, explain.

List any other remarks here.

_____

_____

_____

_____

_____

_____

_____

Signature of investigating police officer: _____

Date: _____

Once all of this information is documented and collected, it should be brought to the lab for a full forensic investigation.

At the lab, there is a log that is signed by the officer dropping off the evidence (see page 40). The evidence then receives a lab identification number. The person accepting the evidence also signs the log to show the transfer of evidence. The evidence is taken to the lab, where it is held in a secure place until it is ready for testing.

When lab technicians open the evidence, they cut the evidence bag open at the end that has not been handsealed. The seal on evidence bags is solid, so they cannot be opened without showing damage to the bag. Once the scientist or technician is done examining the evidence, it is placed back in the bag, and new evidence adhesive tape is placed over the area that has been cut. The scientist must sign and date the tape for verification that he or she was the last one to handle the evidence. Failure to do so could determine the outcome of the verdict.

Also note here that the evidence adhesive tape used for the final seal is delicate. It can easily be broken if not handled with care. This is a safeguard to prevent any kind of tampering. Every time it is opened, it must be resealed with new evidence adhesive tape and signed by the person sealing up the evidence.

Introduction to Subject Matter

(to be read to students)
Approaching a crime scene and filling out reports are some of the most crucial elements of investigating a crime. It can make the difference between evidence admitted into court, not admitted into court, or compromised because of contamination. Sequencing of events in chronological order is not only necessary in the writing process and scientific thought but also relied on heavily in the area of processing a crime scene and setting up a chain of command.

Vocabulary

Algor mortis	The temperature of a body after death, usually taken in the liver or the rectum
Alternate light source	A source that produces different spectrums of light and is measured in nanometers
Amino acid	An organic acid containing one or more amino groups, especially any of a group that make up proteins and are important to living cells
Autolysis	The first stage in decomposition, where anaerobic conditions are created and cells begin to break down
Blanching	Term used in the process of lividity, signified by a white area created by an object underneath the body, usually leaving an impression of the object

Name	Date	Time	Officer no.	Receiver	Date	Time

Department	Signature	Signature

Evidence bag no.	Description of item

Name	Date	Time	Officer no.	Receiver	Date	Time

Department	Signature	Signature

Evidence bag no.	Description of item

Name	Date	Time	Officer no.	Receiver	Date	Time

Department	Signature	Signature

Evidence bag no.	Description of item

Blunt force trauma	Trauma caused to an area of the body from use of an instrument striking the body violently
Cadaveric spasm	Instantaneous rigor mortis in the body, identified by clenched fists in a manner similar to the bench press
Chain of custody	Establishing who enters the crime scene and handles the evidence
CLEAN	Commonwealth Law Enforcement Assistance Network (Pennsylvania)
Control sample	The standard against which the results are compared
Cyanoacrylate	A liquid acrylate monomer belonging to a group with adhesive properties, used in the process of fuming for fingerprints
Drug paraphernalia	Any device used to get drugs into the body
Entrance log	A list of all people entering a crime scene
Fatty acid	An organic acid belonging to a group that may occur naturally as waxes, fats, and essential oils; fatty acids consist of a straight chain of carbon atoms linked by single bonds and ending in a carboxyl group
Gastric content	The food remaining in the stomach after a meal
Hyoid bone	A bone found at the top of the vertebrae, a support or base for the tongue
Ligatures	Marks that appear on the skin from anything used to bind or strangle a person
Livor mortis	The process of blood settling in the body after death; the color of the body changes depending on the time, temperature, and cause of death
Miranda rights	The rights that allow a person to say and do nothing until a lawyer is present
NCIC	National Crime Information Center
Perpetrator	The person who is responsible for committing the crime
Polymer	A natural or synthetic compound that consists of large molecules made of many chemically bonded smaller and identical molecules
Rap sheet	Record of arrests and prosecutions
Rigor mortis	The progressive stiffening of the body that occurs several hours after death; it is due to the coagulation of protein in the muscles
Spent casing	The casing surrounding a projectile; it contains the elements necessary to produce a reaction causing the projectile to be fired
Victim	The person against whom a crime has been committed

42   *Partners in Crime*

CRIME SCENE DO NOT CROSS CRIME SCENE DO NOT CROSS CRIME SCENE DO NOT CROSS CRIME SCENE DO NOT CROSS CRIME SCENE DO NOT CROSS CRIME SCENE DO NOT CROSS CRIME SCENE

Lesson Objectives (with Standards Guide Words)

- Students will learn about the practical application of event sequencing and chronology as they apply to the chain of custody. (Guide words: application, event sequencing, chronology, main idea, details)

- Students will learn about the importance of specificity in describing events through the use of details. (Guide words: main idea, details, evidence, resources)

- Students will explore process-based inquiry through learning the steps involved in approaching a crime scene. (Guide words: inquiry, process learning)

- Students will explore prioritization and outlining through an exercise delving into setting up a chain of command. (Guide words: outline, prioritization)

- Students will learn necessary terminology for understanding certain reports. (Guide words: vocabulary, syntax, semantics)

- Students will learn the sequential steps of processing a crime scene. (Guide words: sequence, order of importance, chronology)

Lesson and Learning Activity

Allotted time: fifty minutes

This is a good time to do a lesson on prepositional phrases. While searching for clues at a burglary, it is imperative that the officer describe where the evidence was found. Give students a list of pieces of evidence that can be found at a burglary. Ask them to use each piece of evidence in a sentence having a prepositional phrase describing where each one was found.

The evidence:

Fingerprints

Shoe prints

Soda bottle

Cigarette butt

Footprints on the door

Pry marks

Gum wrapper

Piece of torn fiber

Twigs and leaves

Now have students draw a picture of the crime scene. Tell them that all of this evidence was found in one room. Have them draw the room and write the sentences in

Crime Scene Procedure 43

CRIME SCENE DO NOT CROSS CRIME SCENE DO NOT CROSS CRIME SCENE DO NOT CROSS CRIME SCENE DO NOT CROSS CRIME SCENE DO NOT CROSS CRIME SCENE DO NOT CROSS CRIME SCENE

their respective places on the picture. Students can add furniture and other items as needed.

In addition, have students use the list to determine which would be the best pieces of evidence and why. You should ask students to list all of them in order from highest importance to lowest. Then have them explain why they think the specific piece of evidence is important. They should think about what kind of clues can be provided by each piece. Then ask students what kind of documentation is necessary for each piece of evidence.

Springboard to Writing

Allotted time: fifty minutes

Choose five students from the class. Assign roles to each individual. Two students should be detectives and one should be a responding officer; the other two students should be suspects. Give students props and costumes so they know who is who. Once the students are in their places, read this scenario to them. Students can act it out as you read the scenario. It works well if you choose students before class and give them a copy of the scenario so they can prepare.

> *On Friday evening, a 911 call was made from Catherine Jersey to the West Falls Police Department. She reported a stabbing over drugs. The responding officer arrived to find a body lying on the ground and people surrounding it. The officer called for backup, an ambulance, and detectives. The ambulance came and could not revive the victim. Therefore, they had to wait for clearance from detectives before they could take the body to the morgue. After the people were cleared, the detectives stepped in to try to make some sense out of the mess. Detectives Gray and Baker wound up with two people. One person was Catherine Jersey, the witness who phoned the police. The other was Dan Odderson (who was the one responsible for the stabbing).*
>
> *Dan realized that the cops already knew that drugs were involved because Catherine had told the police that in her phone call. He decided to tell the truth this time. He explained to detectives that he sold the victim, Todd Pickering, a bag of marijuana. When Todd gave the money to Dan, Dan added it to his already existing wad of bills. Seeing this, Todd pulled out a knife and demanded that Dan hand over all of his money. Dan slapped the knife out of his hand and they began to wrestle. Dan eventually grabbed the knife because Todd had a choke hold on him. Dan stabbed Todd deep in the stomach. They continued to wrestle for several minutes until Todd slowed down and eventually died. That is when Catherine called the cops.*
>
> *Now Detectives Gray and Baker have the task of beginning to fill out required paperwork. Where should they start?*

44   *Partners in Crime*

CRIME SCENE DO NOT CROSS CRIME SCENE DO NOT CROSS CRIME SCENE DO NOT CROSS CRIME SCENE DO NOT CROSS CRIME SCENE DO NOT CROSS CRIME SCENE DO NOT CROSS CRIME SCENE

Students can write on a sheet of paper. Have them number the items as they complete a list of what should be done. This should take about five to eight minutes. Now have students role-play the student answers. Are they doing it correctly? Then have students compare their list with that of the teacher (given next). The activity should not take more than fifteen minutes.

1. Read the Miranda rights to Dan Odderson.
2. Obtain a search-and-seizure form for him to sign so his house and person can be searched further for drugs.
3. Use a checklist for a death scene to document all surroundings and the condition of the body.
4. At the station, Dan will be fingerprinted.
5. Dan and Catherine will each fill out a statement.
6. Dan is allowed his one phone call.

CSI Notebook

Allotted time: twenty-five minutes
Now that students have been exposed to the various forms used, give them this scenario and ask them to write the process of what needs to be done.

> On Friday morning at approximately 2:30 A.M., a man named Lukas Haines was found staggering down the street of a high-class community. The officer stopped her vehicle and approached the man. With bloodshot eyes, he squinted when she shined the bright flashlight in his eyes. She asked him if he was lost and needed directions. The officer asked for some identification, and the man began to run. As he was running, his pockets were jingling, as though they were full of change or something. Eventually, the officer tackled the man on someone's front lawn. She turned him over to cuff him, and gold and silver jewelry came out of his pockets. As she was picking him up off the ground, another police officer arrived and said that he had gotten a call about a burglary taking place two blocks from where the man was walking. The man was taken to the police station.
> What kind of paperwork did the officers fill out? Why?

Assessment

• **Mastery (A).** The student displays the process in sequential order and uses the necessary forms to document all processes involved in the prescribed order.

• **Proficient (B).** Few steps in the sequential process are missed. Also, the student displays some of the necessary paperwork, but not all of it.

Crime Scene Procedure 45

CRIME SCENE DO NOT CROSS CRIME SCENE DO NOT CROSS CRIME SCENE DO NOT CROSS CRIME SCENE DO NOT CROSS CRIME SCENE DO NOT CROSS CRIME SCENE DO NOT CROSS CRIME SCENE

- **Satisfactory (C).** The student lists a few of the requirements in order. Most forms of paperwork are mentioned.
- **Unsatisfactory (D).** The student has no order to the process or forms that are necessary.
- **Insufficient (F).** The student does not write about the process or forms. Student might write about the crime and unrelated topics.

Lesson Accommodations and Modifications

Students who have a difficult time writing things down can explain the process to the teacher. Sometimes verbalizing is better for learning support students. This also helps develop their speaking skills.

ESL students might want to use a tape recorder and explain the process. Play it back and type it on the computer. It can then be translated into English.

For Further Study

You can extend this activity further by having students complete an extra-credit assignment. This chapter lists the necessary forms for police officers. If students are interested, have them pursue the legal aspect of a crime. All kinds of forms are necessary when a case is taken to court. Depending on the crime, certain forms must be filled out and filed. Students may wish to choose a certain crime and research the legal forms used in the judiciary process. The report can then be handed in or presented to the class as an "investigative report."

References

Bard, Mike. *Crime Scene Evidence: A Guide to Recovery and Collection of Evidence.* Temecula, Calif.: Staggs, 2001.

Dix, Jay. *Time of Death, Decomposition, and Identification.* New York: CRC Press, 2000.

Douglas, John, Burgess, Anne, Burgess, Allen, and Ressler, Robert. *Crime Classification Manual.* San Francisco: Jossey-Bass, 1992.

Fisher, Barry. *Techniques of Crime Scene Investigating* (6th ed.). New York: CRC Press, 2000.

Genge, Ngaire. *The Forensic Casebook: The Science of Crime Scene Investigating.* New York: Ballantine, 2002.

Hawthorne, Mike. *First Responder: A Guide to Physical Evidence Collection for Patrol Officers.* New York: CRC Press, 1998.

Lee, Henry. *Henry Lee's Crime Scene Handbook.* Durham, N.C.: Academic Press, 2001.

Randall, Brad. *Death Investigation: The Basics.* Tucson, Ariz.: Galen Press, 1997.

Spitz, Werner. *Spitz and Fisher Medico-Legal Investigation of Death* (3rd ed.). Springfield, Ill.: Charles C. Thomas, 1993.

Chapter Three

Crime Scene Analysis

Overview for Teachers (Blood)

At the crime scene, some evidence can be analyzed on the spot. Investigators have a crime scene kit with various items that can test evidence. Other evidence can be analyzed if the investigator has a background in bloodstain evidence, ballistics, fingerprints, or toolmarks.

There are several presumptive tests that can be used to tell if a stain is blood. One for use in labs or in the field is the KM test, which stands for Kastle-Meyer Reagent test. To make the reagent, you need:

2 grams of phenolphthalein

10 grams of potassium hydroxide

800 milliliters of absolute ethanol

(*Note:* a small amount of zinc metal dust should be added to the solution to keep the clear reagent from turning a pinkish color.)

To determine if a stain might be blood, add one drop of distilled water to the tip of a clean cotton-tipped applicator. Swab the suspect area until some has rubbed off on the applicator. Add one drop of KM reagent and watch for a color change. Then add one drop of 3 percent hydrogen peroxide. Ask students to make note of any color changes. If blood is present, the swab will turn a pinkish color. However weird it may sound, potatoes and horseradish will also give the same result. So, if your school does not allow use of any kind of blood, you can make a mixture with mashed potatoes or creamy horseradish.

Remember that this is only a presumptive test; it is not a positive test for blood. It does not tell whether it is animal or human blood. To do that, a precipitin test is needed. Paul Uhlenhuth, a biologist, found out that if he injected protein from a chicken egg into a rabbit and mixed the serum from the rabbit with egg white, the egg proteins from the liquid would separate into a cloudy substance known as precipitin. For testing purposes, the sample is placed in a

48   *Partners in Crime*

CRIME SCENE DO NOT CROSS CRIME SCENE DO NOT CROSS CRIME SCENE DO NOT CROSS CRIME SCENE DO NOT CROSS CRIME SCENE DO NOT CROSS CRIME SCENE DO NOT CROSS CRIME SCENE

gel on a glass slide next to a sample of the reagent. When an electric current is passed through the glass, the protein molecules filter into the gelatin and toward each other. If or when a line forms where they meet, it is a positive test for human blood. The line where the two meet is called a precipitin line.

Microcrystalline tests are also performed. Tests named after Takayama and Teichmann are two of the most common. These procedures add chemicals to make the blood form crystals with the hemoglobin.

Bloodstain evidence can be one of the most revealing aspects of a crime scene. It can be used to tell the position of people or objects, track their movement through a crime scene, or sequence the events and how the crime unfolded. Blood also contains essential DNA that can be used to convict a criminal. Bloodstain evidence is referred to as blood spatter. This means that blood flows in a predictable pattern when acted upon by an outside force or gravity, or on a surface that comes in contact with blood.

Some criminals try to wipe away with cleaning products. Unfortunately for them, the use of luminol reacts with the hemoglobin in the blood and makes it glow like a firefly. This has proven useful for many crime scene investigators. However, it is not used as much as is seen on television because it degrades the sample that could otherwise be used for DNA extraction. The PCR method can use a sample that has been sprayed with luminol. It also has to be completely dark; if you see your hand in front of your face, it is not dark enough.

Blood spatter analysis yields two valuable pieces of information: the direction in which the blood travels, and the impact angle at which the blood strikes a surface. Surface tension plays a role in how the blood makes a pattern. This is the elastic property of the liquid's surface that makes it tend to contract, caused by the forces of attraction between molecules. Cohesive forces tend to resist penetration and separation. For a blood drop to fall, the gravitational force acting on the blood must exceed its surface tension. Without it, the blood would act like a slime or goo. Finally, surface tension minimizes spattering before impact with a smooth, hard surface, no matter from how high the blood drop falls.

Directionality of a blood drop is usually apparent by finding and identifying the tail of the drop. Blood that strikes a surface at anything less than a perpendicular is elongated, taking on a tear shape. To determine the direction, simply identify the tail of the blood drop—the tail points in the direction of travel.

If the tail is difficult to identify, look for the area where the blood is thicker. Wherever that area is, the opposite side points to the direction of travel.

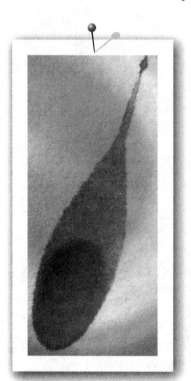

Directionality of Blood Drop, with a Clear Tail Pointing Upward

Blood Drop Without Tail, But with Directionality Toward Left

Crime Scene Analysis

49

CRIME SCENE DO NOT CROSS CRIME SCENE DO NOT CROSS CRIME SCENE DO NOT CROSS CRIME SCENE DO NOT CROSS CRIME SCENE DO NOT CROSS CRIME SCENE DO NOT CROSS CRIME SCENE

Figuring out the impact angle can also be done by measuring the length and width of the drop. The angle of impact is the acute angle formed between the direction of the blood drop and the plane of the surface it strikes. A sine trigonometric function must be used. When measuring the length of the drop, stop where the tail begins. This is the true length of the drop. Use this formula:

$$\sin\angle = width/length$$

Let's say, for example, that a blood drop has a width of 1.5 centimeters and the length is 3 centimeters. The formula looks like this:

$$\sin\angle = 1.5/3$$
$$.5 = \sin\angle; \angle = 30 \text{ degrees}$$

The point of origin and convergence can also be determined. Once the directionality of a group of stains has been set, it is possible to create a two-dimensional point area for the group of stains. Draw a line through the long axis of each of a group of blood drops. Eventually, all of these lines will intersect at the point of convergence.

Introduction to Subject Matter

(to be read to students)

Blood plays a significant role in crime scene investigation. It can be used to collect DNA evidence that can be compared to a suspect sample. Blood also reveals a lot about how the crime happened and where certain events took place. It follows specific patterns consistently when acted upon by an outside force. The speed in which it is struck makes a discernible pattern, as does the height from which it falls. All of these factors are important in figuring out the events at the scene of the crime.

A drop of blood traveling through space toward the ground takes on a spherical shape. As it comes in contact with the ground, it forms a circular pattern if the surface is flat and somewhat smooth. Sometimes the droplet has little splashes on the outside of the circle; this is called a "crowning" effect. When the surface is at an angle to the direction of travel, the pattern changes. A simple experiment can be done to show patterns of blood drops.

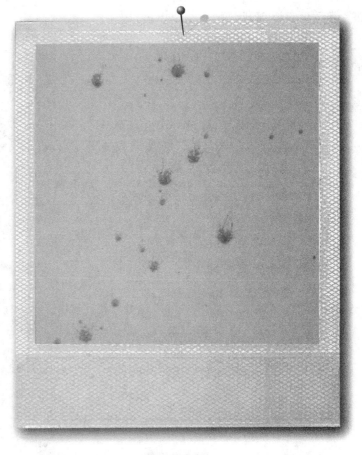

Cast-off Spatter

50   *Partners in Crime*

CRIME SCENE DO NOT CROSS CRIME SCENE DO NOT CROSS CRIME SCENE DO NOT CROSS CRIME SCENE DO NOT CROSS CRIME SCENE DO NOT CROSS CRIME SCENE DO NOT CROSS CRIME SCENE

Blood Drop Falling from 6 Inches onto Sketch Pad Art Paper

From 12 Inches

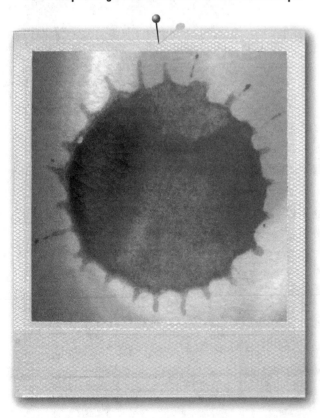

From 24 Inches

From 36 Inches

Crime Scene Analysis   **51**

CRIME SCENE DO NOT CROSS CRIME SCENE DO NOT CROSS CRIME SCENE DO NOT CROSS CRIME SCENE DO NOT CROSS CRIME SCENE DO NOT CROSS CRIME SCENE DO NOT CROSS CRIME SCENE DO NOT CROSS CRIME SCENE

The basic blood drop pattern usually comes from a passive drop. This means blood is dripping without any applied force. This blood drop usually results in a circular pattern with possible crowns on the outside, as seen in the four figures. (*Aside for the teacher:* show figures on page 50 to the students.)

As outside forces act upon or interrupt the flow of the blood, the pattern changes. One is called a "cast off" spatter. This appears when an object is used for the crime; coming into contact with the blood, some of it remains on the instrument. When the instrument is raised into the air for another strike, the speed and force of the instrument causes the blood to fly or cast off the instrument. This pattern is sometimes seen on a ceiling when someone has been beaten or bludgeoned. (*Aside for the teacher:* show the figure on page 49 to the students.)

Another type of spatter is called high-impact. This is made when an instrument is used to beat the victim. When the instrument hits the blood at high speed, it breaks up the blood into a pattern that looks like a spray. (*Aside for the teacher:* show the two figures on this page to the students.)

The next type of pattern is sometimes called an arterial spray. This is caused when a major artery is cut. The first few spurts may shoot up to five or six feet. As more blood is released, it will travel less and less far.

When a gun is used at very close range (a matter of inches), a back spatter

Two Examples of High-Impact Spatter from a Tire Iron

pattern occurs. The impact of the gunshot causes the blood to flow backward—toward the shooter—because of the force of the firearm releasing pressure from the gases in the bullet. This causes blood to land on the clothes of the criminal and even on the inside of the barrel of the gun.

Contact and transfer patterns are also found at crime scenes. Fingerprints, handprints, and foot impressions are found when a bloody part of the body comes in contact with an object or surface. This pattern can also specify the direction in which the victim or perpetrator was moving. (*Aside for the teacher:* show the two figures on page 52 to the students.)

52   *Partners in Crime*

CRIME SCENE DO NOT CROSS CRIME SCENE DO NOT CROSS CRIME SCENE DO NOT CROSS CRIME SCENE DO NOT CROSS CRIME SCENE DO NOT CROSS CRIME SCENE DO NOT CROSS CRIME SCENE DO NOT CROSS CRIME SCENE

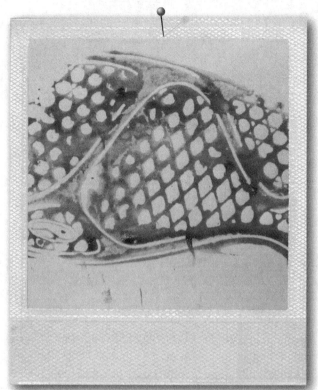

Two Transfer Patterns

If someone is bleeding under his or her clothes and comes into contact with an object or surface pattern, a fabric impression can appear. This can later be matched up with the clothes the victim was wearing (or not wearing). Smudges and smears appear when a bloody object comes in contact with a surface. There have also been cases where someone writes in blood.

Vocabulary

Arterial spray	Bloodstain pattern caused when a major artery or vein is cut open
Ballistics	The study of projectiles and the direction of travel
Blood spatter	The pattern that is created when blood contacts a surface or is acted upon by an outside force
Cast off	The pattern that is created when an instrument covered with blood moves through space at medium to high velocity
Contact pattern	The pattern created when a bloody object or body part comes into contact with a surface
Crowning	Little splashes that appear outside of the circle of a blood drop
Hemoglobin	An iron-containing protein in red blood cells that combines reversibly with oxygen and transports it from the lungs to body tissues

High impact	The pattern created when blood is acted upon by an outside force at high velocity
Impact angle	The angle at which a splash of blood strikes a surface
KM test	Kastle-Meyer test; a presumptive test for all kinds of blood
Luminol	A reagent that reacts with the hemoglobin in the blood and makes it glow
Passive drop	A pattern created when blood contacts a surface traveling under normal (gravitational) conditions
PCR	Polymerase chain reaction, a DNA amplification technique
Smear	A pattern that appears when a bloody object or body part touches a surface
Surface tension	The elastic property of a liquid's surface that makes it tend to contract, caused by the forces of attraction between the molecules

Lesson Objectives (with Standards Guide Words)

- Students will learn the term *bloodstain evidence* and its implications. (Guide words: definition, critical thinking, conclusion, generalization)
- Students will learn the terms for patterns that are created by blood. (Same guide words as in preceding objective)
- Students will learn to determine the angle of impact. (Guide words: length, width, sine)
- Students will learn to determine the origin of a stain. (Guide words: definition, critical thinking, conclusion, generalization)
- Students will be able to determine the directionality of a stain. (Same guide words as in previous objective)
- Students will learn to revise sentences by adding content through the use of various parts of speech. (Guide words: content, detail, adjectives, adverbs, prepositional phrases)

Lessons and Learning Activities: Labs

Allotted time: fifty minutes

The labs given here look at blood evidence in a variety of situations. For this lab, you need:

Cow's blood (700–800 ml; the best alternative to cow's blood is red gel poster paint by Crayola; make a 4–10 percent solution with water)

Pipettes

Simulated evidence item (a pipe, bat, knife, and so on)

Ring stand and clamp

Plain white paper

Cardboard (lots of it)

Rough piece of wood

Protractor and marker

Piece of flat glass

A mop and hot, soapy water

What to Do: Part One

Start with the glass surface. Place it at the base of the stand, clamp in the simulated piece of evidence, and angle it so the direction of flow lands on the glass. The height should be two feet at its lowest point. Using the pipette, begin to add one drop of blood at a time until it drips one or two times from the piece of evidence onto the glass. Have students observe what the pattern looks like. Repeat the same process with the other surfaces (cardboard, paper, and so on). Have students think about how different surfaces affect the type of pattern created.

The purpose of part one is to show that the angle of the simulated piece of evidence does not affect the pattern, but the surface does. It is the surface that must be at an angle to the simulated piece of evidence, as part two shows.

Part Two

Using the cardboard, place it so it can pivot to the right or left. Using a protractor, measure a 10 degree angle. Repeat the process with the simulated weapon and drop blood on it until it drips one time on the cardboard. Have students note the pattern that is created. Use a marker and write 10 degrees under it. After the stain dries, repeat the process, increasing the angle 10 degrees every time. The end result should produce a nice collection of blood drops. Save this sample for a later experiment.

Part Three

Take a long piece of cardboard that is approximately two feet wide by eight feet long. Tape the cardboard to the wall. Using a sample evidence item (pipe, bat, hammer, etc.), soak one end of it in the blood. Once it is done, swing the item in a fast swift motion up along the cardboard. Try one up motion and one down motion. Have students observe the pattern that is made.

Part Four

Tape a new piece of cardboard to the foot of the wall. This piece should be approximately five feet wide and three feet high. Place approximately 100–200 ml of blood on a paper plate on the floor (a floor that can be cleaned up easily) in front of the cardboard. Using a sample item, hit the plate (which is on the floor—or better yet, do this outside) as hard as possible with the object. (This experiment can be quite messy.) The person swinging the object should wear some protective gear like a rain suit to keep himself or herself from getting covered in blood. The outcome pattern will produce a beautiful high-impact spatter pattern.

Again, this can be quite messy, and disagreeable for some students (and teachers). It is highly recommended that you clear this activity with the principal or appropriate authority. Additionally, students should be given the choice of opting out of the activity. There are numerous considerations here to take into account; your anticipation and preparation go far in clearing the way for an effective learning experience. (At the very least, the class can simply look at the pictures and not carry out the activity.)

Part Five

Using the blood-soaked item, have a student walk around the room as the blood drips on the floor. Students should note any differences compared to the drops created in part one.

Part Six

This experiment requires a mop and hot soapy water from your maintenance department. Place approximately 200–300 ml of blood on the floor. Have a student step in the puddle and walk around the room. The student should keep walking until the tracks are not visible anymore. Have students observe the patterns and how they change as the tracks get lighter in appearance.

Part Seven

Repeat the process of part six. This time have the student run instead of walk. Are there any differences in the pattern?

Part Eight

A pint of blood is needed for this one. Pour half of the blood onto a flat surface. Stop, and pour the rest of it into the existing puddle from a height of about two to three feet. This creates a secondary impact spatter.

Flow Patterns and Drying Time

Obviously, gravity affects the flow of blood. How much blood there is determines how far the blood flows and how fast it dries.

Volume and surface type affect drying time, as do the texture and absorption rate. Environmental factors such as temperature, humidity, and air circulation have an effect on how fast or slow blood dries. Blood drops dry from the outside in. As they dry, the color changes from a deep red to a brown rusted color.

Try using other liquid substances. Students should see differences in the patterns that are created from a variety of substances. Which substances run faster and slower? Why is that? (It is because the density of each liquid determines how fast it runs down a surface.)

Springboard to Writing

Allotted time: two class periods

> *On Monday morning, police were called to the scene of a brutal beating. After securing the area, detectives entered the crime scene. On the floor lay a wooden bat covered in blood. The white walls of the kitchen were covered with various bloodstains. The scene was properly documented and the body was taken away. A blood spatter expert was called to the scene to assist in the investigation.*

Think about what bloodstains will be evident given the scenario. Generate a list of the possible patterns that might appear at the scene. Then write an informative essay explaining how each piece of bloodstain evidence was created.

CSI Notebook

Allotted time: fifty minutes

One problem students face is content development through using parts of speech. Depending on the level of the class, ask students which parts of speech can enhance content. Generate a list on the board. If your students are at the level of using adverbial and adjectival clauses, incorporate them into the lesson. Next, have students read the sample essay that follows and revise it so it is more descriptive. Tell students that they will first play the role of the teacher, reading through it, correcting it, and making comments on how it can be improved. Then have them turn writer and rewrite the essay so it is better.

This paper is a documentation piece that an officer put together after working a homicide. The officer has to write a report, part of which is writing a narrative of exactly how he documented everything and what he saw. This paper will be brought up again in the courtroom for everyone to see when testifying. If you were a defense lawyer, what would you do with this paper? Think about what it should look like and rewrite it so it is acceptable.

> *The following is my essay about what I saw at the crime scene. When I came in, I saw a pattern on the wall. It was in the middle of the living room and it was all over the wall. I took a picture or two to document it. I used another light source too, when I took the picture. The crime scene unit then came in to collect the evidence. They placed it in boxes and wrote some stuff on it.*
>
> *Next, I went into the bathroom. On the floor was a puddle of blood. It looked like it was there a while because it was starting to dry around the edges. It was near the tub, and there were some blood spots on the tub. I took some more pictures. Again the crime scene unit came in when I was done and did their thing.*
>
> *As I walked down the hallway, I found small drops on the floor. I think they came from carrying the body in the hallway. The drops were circular. I took pictures and went to the kitchen.*
>
> *In the kitchen, all of the other officers were in there. I gave them my report of what I saw and photographed. They nodded their heads and I left to drop my film off to be developed.*

Assessment

- **Mastery (A).** Student can find all the vague sentences in the sample piece. Student can rewrite the piece in a clear and precise manner that shows vivid description through the use of adjectives, adverbs, and prepositional phrases.
- **Proficient (B).** Student finds most of the vague sentences in the sample piece. The revised paper shows adequate use of adjectives, adverbs, and prepositional phrases.
- **Satisfactory (C).** Student finds a few vague sentences in the sample piece. The revised paper does not show much revision or use of adjectives, adverbs, and prepositional phrases.
- **Unsatisfactory (D).** Student finds one or two vague sentences in the sample piece. The revised paper does not show any revision; it is just a copy of the sample.
- **Insufficient (F).** The student does not revise the sample piece. The revised piece is not completed.

Lesson Accommodations and Modifications

Some students are not sure about the parts of speech and the role they play in developing content. If this is the case, have them try to identify the adjectives, adverbs, and prepositional phrases in the sample piece. Grade them on the number of identifications they make in the sample essay.

For ESL students, remember that their language may differ considerably from English. In some languages, the descriptive words come after instead of before the word described. You should have students rewrite sentences where this is the case.

For Further Study

A lot of students might find this area interesting and wish to conduct more experiments outside of school. You must stress the implications of working with blood in any environment; students should only do so under the strict supervision of an adult who is experienced in working with blood and the implications it poses. Do not use blood unless under adult supervision. Crayola gel poster paint works well enough.

If a person is interested in becoming an expert in the field of blood spatter work, he or she could start out as a law enforcement officer and move on to receive more training in mathematics, physics, and serology. Another way to obtain a job like this would be to earn a bachelor's degree in one of the sciences and complete other courses in mathematics, physics, and serology. On-the-job training is also required.

Overview for Teachers (Gunshot Residue)

Gunshot residue can be found in several places. GSR (gunshot residue) occurs when a firearm is fired at close range. Usually beyond about ten yards, not much GSR appears around the entrance of the projectile, whether it be on a surface, directly on the skin of the victim, or on clothing. As the distance from the shooter increases, the trajectory of the gases and projectile decreases. As the speed of the residue slows, it forms a trajectory or arc.

In a homicide or suicide, there is usually a stippling effect on the skin or clothing. This looks like little dots around the area of the entrance of the bullet. It usually indicates that the gun barrel was not held directly to the skin. Stippling can also be seen on shirts or surface areas where the bullet has entered. Another effect of GSR is when there is direct contact between the skin and the barrel; this usually creates a starring effect. It happens because of "pocketing." The explosion of the gun causes the skin to open and allow the gases inside. The powder fills in the space between the skin and tissue or bone; it actually separates the skin from the tissue. The force and speed cause the skin to rip or tear and produce a star shape on the skin. In instances like this, GSR can be found inside the wound and around the damaged tissue.

Another area to search, in a case like this, is in and around the barrel of the gun. After the shot is fired, a blowback effect is created on the contact surface. A vacuumlike process occurs and the barrel of the gun acts like a vacuum chamber and sucks in tissue material. Under microscopic examination, the tissue can be detected and collected.

The person who fires the gun will be in contact with the gases of the explosion. Until the hand is washed (or time has elapsed), the GSR adheres to the skin. If the person is very active after shooting, the residue can wear off in a matter of four to eight hours. Sometimes even after thorough washing, traces of residue remain behind. Under sources other than natural sunlight, the GSR has a glowing effect. The suspect area can be tested for GSR by using a test kit carried in the crime scene kit and available right on the spot. A swab can also be taken and sent to the lab for identification.

Introduction to Subject Matter

(to be read to students)
Gunshot residue is made up of several powders that ignite when charged by a spark. The spark is usually created when the firing pin hits the bottom casing of the bullet. As a projectile leaves the barrel of a gun, the residue is spread into the air and lands on surfaces that are within close proximity of the barrel. Gunshot residue may land on clothing, hands, other body parts, and whatever else is in proximity to the gun barrel. It can be identified through several tests. Sometimes an alternative light source can be used to expose gunshot residue that might not appear under normal lighting conditions.

Vocabulary

Blowback effect	The result of close or direct contact on the skin; tissue and blood particles appear in and around the barrel of the gun
GSR	Gunshot residue; any residue that is left on a surface after a gun is fired
Pocket	Separation of skin from tissue and bone due to the explosion of gases when a gun is fired in direct contact with the skin

Crime Scene Analysis   **59**

CRIME SCENE DO NOT CROSS CRIME SCENE DO NOT CROSS CRIME SCENE DO NOT CROSS CRIME SCENE DO NOT CROSS CRIME SCENE DO NOT CROSS CRIME SCENE DO NOT CROSS CRIME SCENE

Starring effect	A result from the tearing of skin from a direct-contact gunshot; the opening looks like a star
Stippling	A result of a close-range gunshot; the GSR appears on the surface as little dots

Lesson Objectives (with Standards Guide Words)

- Students will learn what makes gunshot residue. (Guide words: gunshot residue, powders)
- Students will learn specific terms describing projectile and wound effects. (Guide words: blowback, pocket, starring, stippling)
- Students will learn to identify gunshot residue through chemical analysis. (Guide words: chemical analysis)
- Students will learn to use alternative light sources to identify gunshot residue. (Guide words: alternative light sources)
- Students will learn to identify direct objects. (Guide words: direct object, noun, pronoun, verb)
- Students will learn to identify indirect objects. (Guide words: indirect object, noun, pronoun, verb)

Lesson and Learning Activity

Allotted time: fifty minutes

On Friday night, June 13, 2003, a drive-by shooting occurred in the downtown area of East Pikeland. Three people were killed and two were injured. Police arrived at the scene and found spent bullet casings on the ground in the middle of the street. While the EMT crews took care of the injured and dead, the police were busy securing the area, marking out the shell casings on the ground, and taking pictures. The police collected the evidence and sent it to the crime lab for identification. It was determined that the casings were from a 9mm gun.

Police were sure that it was a gang-related shooting. The dead were members of a gang, and bystanders said that the car was full of members from a rival gang. One person did get a make on the license plate of the car (a 2001 red Honda Accord)—a vanity plate that read GNG BNGR (as in "gang banger"). Police found out that the car was registered to a Stephen Wolf. He had a rap sheet a mile long with priors for assault, possession of drugs, weapons, and grand theft larceny.

Police made a visit to his house to question him. He denied ever being in the neighborhood the night of the shooting. He stated he was hanging with his homies Greg, Jay, and Robert. Police noticed a bulge in the

60   *Partners in Crime*

CRIME SCENE DO NOT CROSS CRIME SCENE DO NOT CROSS CRIME SCENE DO NOT CROSS CRIME SCENE DO NOT CROSS CRIME SCENE DO NOT CROSS CRIME SCENE DO NOT CROSS CRIME SCENE

right-hand side of his shirt. It revealed a 9mm gun. (He had a permit to carry it.) Police did not have a warrant, so they could not get the gun. Instead they went looking for his homies to verify the story.

Of course, all of his buddies, who also have long rap sheets, backed up his story. With nothing further for them, police went back to the neighborhood to question the witnesses to the shooting. One member of the gang said he could definitely identify Stephen and two of the other boys. Police considered this enough to get a search warrant for the four suspects.

Police went to Stephen first and took his gun as evidence. He was arrested and brought in for questioning. His other three buddies were also picked up and brought into the station. Greg and Jay too owned 9mm guns. All three weapons were sent to the crime lab for firearm identification tests with the suspect casings found at the crime scene. (This lab is conducted in Chapter Twelve.)

Along with the arrest warrant, police collected the clothes that each suspect was wearing the night of the shooting. Not knowing why the clothes were needed, the boys turned over their shirts. Jay had a dark blue button-down shirt. Greg and Stephen were both wearing black t-shirts. Robert had a white t-shirt.

For the teacher:

Find articles of clothing that resemble these shirts. If you do not have access to gunpowder, you may use a small amount of any kind of powder that fluoresces. Sprinkle some on just one of the shirts. Using an ultraviolet light, turn out the room lights and wave the UV source over each shirt. Have students note any observations made. Next, have students wear a pair of orange goggles. Wave the UV light over the shirts again and have students note any observations. Repeat the same process with red goggles, and then yellow. Students will see that different-colored goggles create varying colors of reflection from the shirt. The shirt that has the gunshot residue on it will belong to Stephen Wolf.

If you have access to a car with vinyl seats, powder can be placed on areas of the seat to determine where the shooter was sitting. The alternative light source or GSR kits can be used. These packages can be purchased through a crime scene product company.

If the funding is not available, you can use this lab to conduct a test for GSR. Here are the supplies you will need:

Copper sample

Nickel sample

Lead sample

Filter paper cut into two-inch squares

DTO (dithiooximide) reagent

10 percent ammonium hydroxide

Small tray for submerging squares

Pipettes

Iron or hot plate

A nonporous surface

For the students to do:

1. Cut filter paper into two-inch squares.
2. Soak the squares with the ammonium hydroxide.
3. After putting on a pair of gloves, press the square firmly on the suspect area.
4. Add the DTO reagent (two or three drops) on the suspect area.
5. Place on the hot plate until almost dry.
6. Upon completion of the drying process, note any changes that have occurred. What consistencies are there between samples? What are the differences?

GSR with Lead

You'll need these supplies:

Known lead sample

Filter paper cut into two-inch squares

Sodium rhodizonate reagent

15 percent acetic acid

Pipettes

For the students to do:

1. Cut filter paper into two-inch squares.
2. Soak them with the acetic acid.
3. After putting on gloves, press the square firmly on the suspect area.
4. Add the sodium rhodizonate.
5. What are the results of the experiment?

If a camera is available, pictures of the process may be taken for display throughout the classroom or posted on your Web site.

Springboard to Writing

Allotted time: twenty-five minutes

A *complement* is a word or group of words that complete the meaning of a verb. They come in two forms: direct objects and indirect objects. A direct object is a noun or pronoun that receives the action of a verb; it completes the meaning of a transitive verb. (A transitive verb is an action verb that directs an action toward a person or thing.) An indirect object is a noun or pronoun that usually comes between the verb and the direct object (but not always: "She gave a present to her sister"); it tells us to whom or for whom or for what the action of the verb is done. It also completes the meaning of a transitive verb; when there is an indirect object then the direct object appears in the sentence as well. Use the scenario given here with the sentences provided.

On Thursday morning, an officer responded to a call from a distressed woman. She said that there was a gang-related shooting going on outside her house. Upon arrival, shots were still being fired. Two bullets struck the police car, in the rear of the vehicle. The officer immediately got out of her car and drew her revolver. She was using a special Smith & Wesson made to fight druglords (it fired special bullets designed to impair but not kill). She managed to catch one of the shooters and detain him.

The crime scene was processed and evidence was collected. The officer was a little shaken up, but she was going to be fine.

A reporter approached her and began to ask her questions. Here is a list of the reporter's notes. Identify the direct and indirect objects in these sentences.

1. *Smith & Wesson made a special handgun for police to use against drug lords.*
2. *The gun fired bullets that were designed to impair the suspect.*
3. *The suspect shot two rounds into the trunk of the car.*
4. *This made her duck down in the seat to avoid the bullets.*
5. *She detained a suspect trying to flee the scene.*
6. *The tight cuffs gave him a mark on his wrists.*
7. *At the lab, scientists will fire the gun for a comparison to the sample projectile.*
8. *Scientists will match the lands and grooves from the sample and fired projectiles.*
9. *A scientist can use his UV light to detect gunshot residue on clothing too.*
10. *The scientist will explain his results to the jury when the trial starts.*

Answers:

1. Smith & Wesson made a special <u>handgun</u> (direct object) for police to use against drug lords.
2. The gun fired <u>bullets</u> (direct object) that were designed to impair the suspect.
3. The suspect shot two <u>rounds</u> (direct object) into the trunk of the car.
4. This made <u>her</u> (indirect object) duck down in the seat to avoid the bullets.
5. She detained a <u>suspect</u> (direct object) trying to flee the scene.
6. The tight cuffs gave <u>him</u> (indirect object) a <u>mark</u> (direct object) on his wrists.

Crime Scene Analysis

63

CRIME SCENE DO NOT CROSS CRIME SCENE DO NOT CROSS CRIME SCENE DO NOT CROSS CRIME SCENE DO NOT CROSS CRIME SCENE DO NOT CROSS CRIME SCENE DO NOT CROSS CRIME SCENE

7. At the lab, scientists will fire the <u>gun</u> (direct object) for a comparison to the sample projectile.

8. Scientists will match the <u>lands and grooves</u> (direct object) from the sample and fired projectiles.

9. The scientist gave <u>him</u> (indirect object) an <u>UV light</u> (direct object) to detect gunshot residue on the suspect's clothing.

10. The scientist will tell <u>her</u> (indirect object) the <u>results</u> (direct object) when the tests are finished.

CSI Notebook

Allotted time: fifteen minutes

Have students think about the hard evidence that is produced through gunshot residue testing. It can find a definitive match to a shooter (and even the brand of bullets, with some certainty). Students should think about how students and people get away with things by lying. Situations like this occur every day in and out of school. Ask students how life would be different if schools were allowed to investigate situations and use forensic science to help solve them! How would school life be different? What kinds of changes would be evident throughout the school? Is this something the students are for or against? Have them write their personal opinion.

For Further Study

If students are interested in finding out more about gunshot residue, they should contact the local police department. Those professionals can better answer questions, and maybe even refer students to a local crime lab where gunshot residue is analyzed.

If a person is interested in becoming a gunshot residue expert, he or she needs a bachelor's degree in one of the sciences, preferably chemistry. A degree in forensic science with a focus on criminalistics would work too. On-the-job training in the crime lab then takes place for a few years until he or she is ready to go to work in this area.

Cumulative Mystery

Allotted time: forty-five minutes

A continuing mystery appears in several chapters of this book.

> *On 9:00 Tuesday morning, police were called by a letter carrier in Dauphin County. He was delivering his mail and noticed a rancid smell coming from the home of Jackie Morrin. She lived on the corner of Simpson and Lee. She had just built a new house; the dirt roads were still muddy. Police*

64   *Partners in Crime*

CRIME SCENE DO NOT CROSS CRIME SCENE DO NOT CROSS CRIME SCENE DO NOT CROSS CRIME SCENE DO NOT CROSS CRIME SCENE DO NOT CROSS CRIME SCENE DO NOT CROSS CRIME SCENE

arrived on the scene at 9:10. The responding officer immediately notified the detectives and coroner. As he entered the house, he found a body lying on the floor. There was one bullet casing on the floor, from a .45. It looked like a possible suicide, but investigators must make sure to cover all areas to rule out a homicide.

After the crime scene was secured, investigators began to identify and collect the evidence. The gun was placed in an evidence bag and labeled by the detective. The door looked as if it had been pried open with some sort of instrument. They did notice a picture of Jackie and a man who appeared to be her boyfriend. The frame was shattered on the floor and the picture cut in half. Investigators photographed the picture before collecting it. As they looked around the outside of the house, they noticed some tire tracks in the mud. Some of the tracks matched the tires on the police cars, some the mail truck, some matched Jackie's car, and one set of tracks was unknown. These tire tracks were sprayed with hairspray to harden the track and then cast in dental stone. Investigators had their first piece of information to go on. What kind of tire is it, and how will they trace it?

Casting Tire Tracks

Casting tire tracks is a great way to show an endothermic reaction. Dental stone puts out an enormous amount of heat when mixed with water.

Dental stone is the best for this purpose because it gives the most detailed outcome. Plaster of Paris can be used, but it lacks the clarity of dental stone. Dental stone can be ordered from any crime scene supply company, or a dental supply business. If your budget is limited, contact a dental lab; they should be more than willing to donate a couple of pounds for your students. Explain the experiment to the person providing the dental stone, and invite him or her in to observe or even speak about their profession and why dental stone is used.

As in real life, crimes are not solved in a day, as on TV. They take months or even years, and some are never solved. The fact that children have to wait gives them a sense of the amount of patience that is needed for an investigation.

Start with this scenario, and a tire track lab to kick it off. The toughest part of this task might be acquiring a tire. You can contact local tire stores in your area. Ask them if they would like to donate a tire or a piece of tread for use in school. Some places might be reluctant to give away a new tire but will not hesitate to give up a used one.

Along with the tire, tire catalogues are needed for students to use as a reference in the room when identifying the tire. The store may be able to furnish some catalogues, but contacting the manufacturer directly for a class set of catalogues might prove more helpful. Also, acquire some other tire catalogues to see if there are any similarities or differences.

Along with this lab, you need some materials:

One-gallon Ziploc bag

Approximately two pounds of dental stone

Four strips of cardboard

Dirt or soil

Hairspray (extra-hold, like Aquanet)

Cut two of the strips into twelve-inch lengths and make the other two eight inches in length. These should be placed around the tire track to prevent leakage of the dental stone.

If no field is available in which to make the actual impression (which is usually the case), you can purchase an aluminum tray, approximately 17 inches by 11 inches.

Next, find or purchase some fresh dirt for the tire imprint. Potting soil works, but do not buy the kind with pieces of Styrofoam in it. That makes it harder to see the tracks and can be difficult to photograph. Brown dirt gives the best results and is easiest to photograph.

The last item needed is hairspray. The best kind to use is one with maximum hold! Spray it on the area to be cast, and then let it dry. This hardens the soil and holds the dirt in place while performing the cast. It also keeps the soil from sticking to the dental stone. Make sure the mixture is slushy rather than lumpy; lumpy casts do not lie well and do not fill in all of the desired areas. Slushy dental stone still dries all the same and fills in the little nooks and crannies of the tire.

The activity given here should take approximately one class period, though the cast might not be completely dry until the next day. Do not remove the case until the top is totally dry.

Directions for Casting the Imprint

1. Take pictures of the tire track from several angles:

   What differences do you notice depending on the angle?

   Can you use lighting angles to create a better picture?

   Which looks better: color, or black and white? (Black and white gives the better texture.)

2. Add water to the dental stone until it becomes slushy. For a good cast, use about two pounds of mix. What happens to the dental stone after a few minutes? Do you know what kind of reaction this is? What else could you use to cast this impression? Why do you think dental stone is the best?

3. After the stone cast dries, you can lift it and place it in an evidence bag, which is then properly labeled. It should be sealed with evidence tape and signed by the "officer" who cast the print.

4. Now you have the task of searching for the make and brand of the tire. How should you approach this? Where would you find information? Whom should you call?

More information will be forthcoming in the future as more evidence is discovered at the crime scene.

After students have determined the make and model of the tire, they need to find out who sells the tire and how many have been sold recently. Investigators would visit

66   *Partners in Crime*

CRIME SCENE DO NOT CROSS CRIME SCENE DO NOT CROSS CRIME SCENE DO NOT CROSS CRIME SCENE DO NOT CROSS CRIME SCENE DO NOT CROSS CRIME SCENE DO NOT CROSS CRIME SCENE

the stores in the area that are known to have sold that type of tire. They ask how many people have purchased such a tire, who has done so at that store, and so on. It is not necessary for students to call tire stores for information that is fictional; have them hold onto the information about the identity of the tire until they get to the part of the investigation where they will be able to conduct interviews with suspects and read their files.

References

Bevel, Tom, and Gardner, Ross. *Bloodstain Pattern Analysis: With an Introduction to Crime Scene Reconstruction* (2nd ed.). New York: CRC, 2001.

Conklin, Barbara G., Gardner, Robert, and Shortelle, Dennis. *Encyclopedia of Forensic Science.* Phoenix: Oryx, 2002.

DeMaio, Vincent. *Gunshot Wounds: Practical Aspects of Firearms, Ballistics, and Forensic Techniques.* New York: CRC, 1998.

Genge, Ngaire. *The Forensic Casebook: The Science of Crime Scene Investigation.* New York: Ballantine, 2002.

Lee, Henry, and O'Neill, Thomas. *Cracking Cases: The Science of Solving Crimes.* New York: Prometheus, 2002.

Nickell, John. *Crime Science: Methods of Forensic Detection.* Lexington: University Press of Kentucky, 1999.

Owen, David. *Hidden Evidence.* Richmond Hill, Ontario: Firefly Books, 2000.

Schwoeble, A. J., and Exline, David. *Current Methods in Forensic Gunshot Residue Analysis.* New York: CRC, 2000.

Spitz, Werner. *Spitz and Fisher Medico-Legal Investigation of Death* (3rd ed.). Springfield, Ill.: Charles C. Thomas, 1993.

Stuart, James. *Interpretation of Bloodstain Evidence* (2nd ed.). New York: CRC, 2000.

Stuart, James. *Scientific and Legal Applications of Bloodstain Pattern Interpretation.* New York: CRC, 1998.

Wonder, Anita. *Blood Dynamics.* Durham, N.C.: Academic Press, 2001.

Zonderman, John. *Beyond the Crime Lab.* Hoboken, N.J.: Wiley, 1999.

Chapter Four

Fingerprint Analysis

Overview for Teachers

Fingerprints are unique to every individual. They have been used for many years to identify suspects at crime scenes. They actually go down to the dermis portion of the skin; because of this, there is no way to erase your fingerprint. Criminals have been known to scrape their fingers with sharp knives; the prints grow back. They have tried to burn them; they grow back. The more fingers are mutilated, the more unique they become. The only way to erase your fingerprint is to cut your finger off and throw it away.

Another interesting aspect of fingerprints is that they can be taken from a corpse. When decomposition enters the bloating stage, the gases actually separate the skin from the muscle. This is called skin slippage. The detective or examiner can slip the skin off, place it on his or her hand like a glove, and fingerprint the corpse for identification.

Fingerprints appear early on in the development of a child. Around six weeks, the hand looks almost like a paddle. This is when skin is beginning to form around the first joint of the finger, called volar pads. (Volar refers to the palm of the hand or sole of the foot.) Around thirteen weeks, the ridges begin to form in the epidermis layer of the skin. It continues until it grows to the dermis level of the skin. These are the two areas of skin that examiners are concerned with.

Latent print is a phrase that surfaces all the time in crime scene shows on TV. The word *latent* is from Latin, meaning "hidden." It means they are not visible to the naked eye. To bring forth the print for the naked eye, some kind of physical or chemical processing must be used.

Fingerprints are made when a person contacts an area. There are glands in your body that secrete oils and sweat, though most of the print is made up of water. The nature and life of a fingerprint depends on elements such as temperature, light, relative humidity, and precipitation.

If a print is located by the naked eye, it is considered a patent print. These may be found if the person has placed a hand in grease, blood, dirt, and so on. Other prints can show up in the form of impressions—if the person pushed a hand into an area that is impressionable, then it will show.

There are several kinds of fingerprints. Where your volar pads develop determines what kind of fingerprint you have. Low pads usually form into some

68   *Partners in Crime*

CRIME SCENE DO NOT CROSS CRIME SCENE DO NOT CROSS CRIME SCENE DO NOT CROSS CRIME SCENE DO NOT CROSS CRIME SCENE DO NOT CROSS CRIME SCENE DO NOT CROSS CRIME SCENE

Arch

type of arch pattern. High pads generally make a type of whorl pattern, and pads in the middle typically result in a loop-type pattern.

Arches come in the form of a plain arch and a tented arch.

Loops come in two forms also, ulnar and radial. The ulnar loop flows in the direction of the little finger; the radial loop flows in the direction of the thumb. (See page 69, top.)

Whorls come in many forms—plain, central pocket loop, double loop, and accidental. (See page 69, bottom.)

Have a local detective come in with the crime scene kit. He or she can fingerprint all of the kids on the same sheets they use for criminals. Once they are printed, students can learn about the patterns of fingerprints, and how to compare them under a magnifier. Have students use the sheets of their fingerprints.

Remember, the computer does not match the prints; it takes a professional fingerprint examiner to make the match. The computer usually offers the ten closest matches and the examiner does the rest. The computer system that is used is called AFIS (Automated Fingerprint Identification System). It is used across the country and around the world. At crime scenes, all the people present are fingerprinted to avoid confusion with prints of the suspect or victim.

There has been controversy about how many points should be sufficient for a match. Some departments use six, others use twelve. Ask your local detective how many points they use for a match. (There can be on average 150 on a full print, depending on the size of the print.)

When students are finished being fingerprinted, the detective can also show them how to lift fingerprints from a crime scene. The detective usually has the necessary materials to complete the task. Then students can compare the lifted prints with those on the fingerprint sheets. The detective should also be able to provide more information about fingerprint charts that they use at the station. The activity should take approximately one class period. If the class is large, break it into two parts: printing and identifying, and dusting and lifting.

Introduction to Subject Matter

(to be read to students)

Fingerprints are individual to every person. No two prints are alike. The more a person tries to change the shape of a print, the more unique it becomes. They also grow back. There are many ways in which a fingerprint can be discovered at a crime scene; a surface can be dusted with powder, fumed with superglue, sprayed, or exposed with special lighting techniques. Prints are then lifted using lifting tape of some kind and

Fingerprint Analysis

69

CRIME SCENE DO NOT CROSS CRIME SCENE DO NOT CROSS CRIME SCENE DO NOT CROSS CRIME SCENE DO NOT CROSS CRIME SCENE DO NOT CROSS CRIME SCENE DO NOT CROSS CRIME SCENE

eventually photographed. Prints must be photographed with a one-to-one lens so when it goes through AFIS it can be matched up with a group of similar prints. The job of the print examiner is to decide on the match of the print. The computer does not make the match; it only provides prints that are similar. In this lesson you will learn the categories of prints and how they can be identified.

Vocabulary

AFIS	Automated Fingerprint Identification System
Amino acid	An organic compound that forms the base of proteins
Fuming	The process of using cyanoacrylate to develop latent prints
Latent prints	Fingerprints that cannot be seen by the naked eye
Patent prints	Fingerprints that are visible to the naked eye
Volar pads	The pads that eventually develop into fingerprints

Lesson Objectives (with Standards Guide Words)

- Students will learn how fingerprints are made. (Guide words: process, research, analysis, synthesis, definition)
- Students will learn the types of fingerprints. (Guide words: classification, comparison, contrast, definition)
- Students will learn the difference between "latent" and "patent" prints. (Guide words: comparison, contrast)
- Students will learn how to lift fingerprints from a surface. (Guide words: analysis, evidence, sequencing, main idea, details)
- Students will learn to identify patterns. (Guide words: definition, experiential learning, analysis, evidence, sequencing, main idea, details)

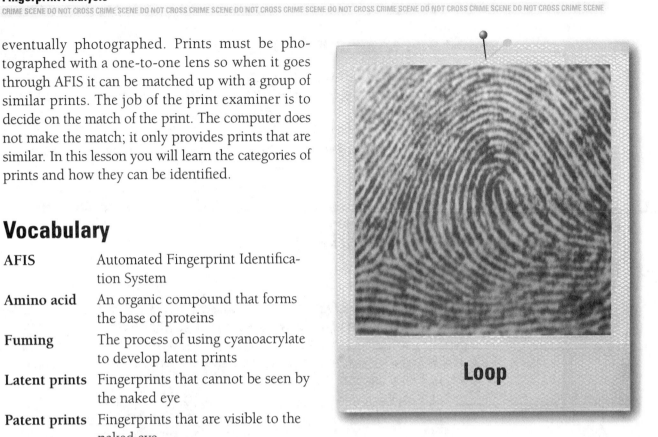

Loop

Whorl

70

Partners in Crime

CRIME SCENE DO NOT CROSS CRIME SCENE DO NOT CROSS CRIME SCENE DO NOT CROSS CRIME SCENE DO NOT CROSS CRIME SCENE DO NOT CROSS CRIME SCENE DO NOT CROSS CRIME SCENE

Lesson and Learning Activity

Allotted time: ninety minutes

Use the fingerprint lab with detectives as the learning activity. Students will then have a basic understanding of fingerprints and the role they play in a crime scene. Encourage students to ask questions about specific details used in identifying a print. The detective who is trained in identifying fingerprints can furnish detailed information about finding specific characteristics in one type of print. Also, have the detective explain the process of keeping the integrity of the evidence throughout the collection process.

Springboard to Writing

Allotted time: fifty minutes

> *On Monday morning, Detective Tomasco received a letter from the judge asking him to appear in court to explain what he did at the crime scene where a murder happened. He specializes in fingerprints, so one of the attorneys is asking him to appear and provide the details of how he discovered and collected (lifted) the print. His testimony is extremely important because the fingerprint he found was the only piece of evidence at the crime scene. It was a latent print on the outside window of the victim's first-floor apartment.*
>
> *Play the role of Detective Tomasco and prepare a one-page informative paper recounting all the steps taken from the time the crime scene was entered to the time the print was submitted into evidence. (Aside for teacher: Use the assessment in this chapter for grading.)*

CSI Notebook

Allotted time: thirty minutes

Have students write a summary of all of the information they have learned about fingerprints. Encourage students to draw pictures where necessary. This entry will take four or five pages. Allow students to use handouts and notes from the fingerprint lab.

Assessment

- **Mastery (A).** Student has focus throughout entire paper. Student uses detailed information from the handouts and follows the correct procedure for lifting a print.
- **Proficient (B).** Student has focus throughout a majority of the paper. Student uses adequate details from the handouts and uses most of the steps to lift a print.
- **Satisfactory (C).** Student does not stay on topic throughout the paper. Student uses limited details from the handouts and uses a few steps for lifting a print.
- **Unsatisfactory (D).** Student talks about the crime, not the suspects. Student uses minimal details from the handouts and does not use any steps for lifting a print.
- **Insufficient (F).** Student writes one paragraph. Student writes about the crime and has nothing to do with lifting a print.

Fingerprint Analysis

71

CRIME SCENE DO NOT CROSS CRIME SCENE DO NOT CROSS CRIME SCENE DO NOT CROSS CRIME SCENE DO NOT CROSS CRIME SCENE DO NOT CROSS CRIME SCENE DO NOT CROSS CRIME SCENE

Lesson Accommodations and Modifications

Students who are not proficient writers may not be able to complete this activity. Instead of writing an essay, have them create a graphic organizer that uses pieces of information rather than sentences. This allows the students to list steps involved in the process of lifting a print.

ESL learners might have a difficult time writing these steps. Use a tape recorder and have them record what they want to say in their own language. Then have them listen to the recording and translate it into English.

For Further Study

If students are interested in doing more research on fingerprints, have them fingerprint their brothers and sisters at home and teach them how to identify their own fingerprints. Also, any kind of transparent tape can be used for lifting prints. Washable ink is the best for creating prints that can be lifted. Ink pads can be purchased at most local arts and crafts or office supply stores.

A latent print examiner should have a four-year degree in forensic science with a focus on criminalistics, criminal justice, or physical science. On-the-job training is usually provided at a crime lab. Eventually, the person needs to be certified by the International Association for Identification.

Cumulative Mystery

Allotted time: fifty minutes

Although students have matched up the tire tracks, they have not been matched to a certain car yet, so the hunt for the suspect continues.

Meanwhile, back at the crime scene, investigators are ready to dust for prints. All other evidence has been properly collected and tagged. Doorways and the room of the crime scene are dusted for prints. Several prints surface from the magnetic powder; they are on the walls, windows, and phone. All prints are lifted and sent to the lab for processing.

Using the fingerprint charts, have students identify the types of fingerprints. Have them document their findings. If your school has the available technology, use a camera to take pictures. If funding allows, a one-to-one lens can be purchased for excellent photos. This way students have a perfect replica, and you do not have to create as many prints. If shooting on a digital camera, and the software allows, print it in black and white. Also have prepared prints from the victim. These can be used for comparisons to the prints lifted.

Create prints from several of the suspects. Try to use the teachers' lounge or a room that can be staged to look like a room in a house. (You can plant the prints in specific areas. Have the prints match the suspects and the victim.)

If so desired, you can use your own prints and those of a colleague. Make sure the areas used are cleaned first to prevent other prints from showing up.

Obtain fingerprint sheets from the police, and fingerprint the suspects and victim. This way, students will have something for comparison. Yes, fingerprint powder is messy, but it wipes off with soap and water. Students should end up with a majority of the prints matching to the victim and two or three that match the suspects listed in Chapter Six. Then tell students that more information will be forthcoming.

Make sure students file this lab where it can be easily retrieved. Have them leave it in a special place in the room or make a folder for each class. You should prepare the prints and print cards before the activity begins.

References

Beavan, Colin. *Fingerprints.* New York: Hyperion, 2001.

Conklin, Barbara G., Gardner, Robert, and Shortelle, Dennis. *Encyclopedia of Forensic Science.* Phoenix: Oryx, 2002.

Edwards, Martin. *Urge to Kill.* Cincinnati: Writers Digest Books, 2002.

Houck, Max. *Mute Witness: Trace Evidence Analysis.* Durham, N.C.: Academic Press, 2001.

Krupowicz, Thomas. *Fingerprints: Innocence or Guilt—The Identity Factors.* Palos Heights, Ill.: Terk Books, 2001.

Lee, Henry, and O'Neill, Thomas. *Cracking Cases: The Science of Solving Crimes.* New York: Prometheus, 2002.

Miller, Hugh. *What the Corpse Revealed: Murder and the Science of Forensic Detection.* New York: St. Martin's Press, 1999.

Nickell, John. *Crime Science: Methods of Forensic Detection.* Lexington: University Press of Kentucky, 1999.

Owen, David. *Hidden Evidence.* Richmond Hill, Ontario: Firefly Books, 2000.

Chapter Five

Blood Typing

Overview for Teachers

Blood typing works on the ABO system. The letters A and B represent the various antigens found in the blood. A red blood cell can be covered with one antigen, both, or neither depending on the type of blood. There are four types of blood, as seen in this table.

Blood Type	Name of Antigens
A	A
B	B
AB	AB
O	None

In red blood cells, antibodies are produced by the immune system to fight foreign material in the body, mainly bacteria and other harmful material. If a person has type A, then the cells contain type B antibodies. If the blood type is B, obviously the blood will have the A antibodies. If the blood type is AB, then no antibodies are present; if the blood type is O, both antibodies are present.

To test for blood type, an antiserum must be used. This can be purchased through a local chemical supply or science company. What happens is that the anti-B antigens are shaped to fit with type B antigens. Therefore, when they are placed together they clump. This is one way to test for a blood type. Using the following table, you can see the results of the antiserum.

74   *Partners in Crime*

CRIME SCENE DO NOT CROSS CRIME SCENE DO NOT CROSS CRIME SCENE DO NOT CROSS CRIME SCENE DO NOT CROSS CRIME SCENE DO NOT CROSS CRIME SCENE DO NOT CROSS CRIME SCENE

Blood Type	Antiserum	Results
A	A	Clumps
B	B	Clumps
AB	AB	Clumps
O	O	No clumps

This table works well in conjunction with the earlier table to give students two ways to look at blood typing.

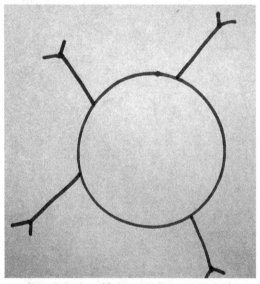

Type A Antigen (Schematic Representation)

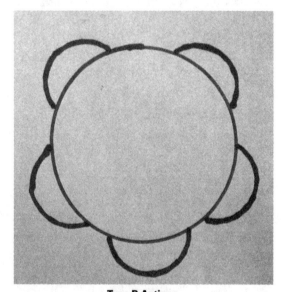

Type B Antigen

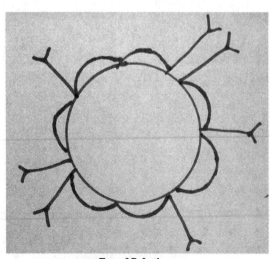

Type AB Antigen

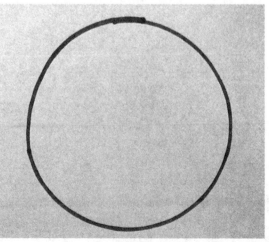

Type O Antigen

Introduction to Subject Matter

(to be read to students)

Although blood typing is used in identifying and matching blood sources at a crime scene, a DNA profile is usually then developed from the suspect source. Blood typing can be used in court, but it is only circumstantial.

Blood typing works on the ABO system. Blood types are A, B, AB, or O. The antigens in your blood determine the blood type you have.

Vocabulary

A	A human blood type of the ABO system, containing the A antigen
B	A human blood type of the ABO system, containing the B antigen
ABO	A human blood type of the ABO system, containing all three antigens
Blood typing	Any class into which human blood is divided for transfusion purposes according to the presence or absence of genetically determined antigens that determine its immunological compatibility

Lesson Objectives (with Standards Guide Words)

- Students will learn the term *blood typing* and incorporate such distinctions into writing and analysis. (Guide words: analysis, evidence, sequencing, main idea, details)

- Students will learn the ABO system and incorporate such distinctions into writing and analysis. (Guide words: analysis, evidence, sequencing, main idea, details, definition)

- Students will identify antigens and incorporate such distinctions into writing and analysis. (Guide words: analysis, evidence, sequencing, main idea, details, writing)

Lesson and Learning Activity

Allotted time: sixty minutes

For the science teacher: these items can be ordered through any science product company:

> Three collection specimens of blood samples
>   from the suspects; label them 1, 2, 3 on slides
>
> Microscope
>
> Antiserum
>
> Dropper

76 *Partners in Crime*

CRIME SCENE DO NOT CROSS CRIME SCENE DO NOT CROSS CRIME SCENE DO NOT CROSS CRIME SCENE DO NOT CROSS CRIME SCENE DO NOT CROSS CRIME SCENE DO NOT CROSS CRIME SCENE DO NOT CROSS CRIME SCENE

The Case of the Foot

On Sunday morning, June 13, 2004, a woman returned from her weekend visit with her sister in Lincoln, Nebraska. She opened the door to a disheveled house, with furniture flipped over and glass smashed on the floor. Alarmed that somebody was still in the house, she called police. When they arrived on the scene and checked the house, no one was found. This was the fourth robbery in the last month in the neighborhood.

It appears that the robber entered through the back door. It had four glass panels, and one pane was shattered all over the floor. Inside the house was one partially exposed muddy shoeprint.

There was also a trail of blood drops through the kitchen to the down-stairs bathroom. The burglar must have wrapped some tissue around the wound.

After interviewing the woman, police discovered that all of her jewelry had been stolen from the safe in her room (behind a rather large Claude Monet painting). While interviewing her, the crime scene unit arrived to col-lect evidence. They began at the back door with the point of entry and established that the door was kicked in forcefully, breaking off the deadbolt lock. The blood was swabbed, dried, and placed in a little brown box that was labeled. They dusted for fingerprints, but nothing showed up. However, they did find a partial shoeprint on the door. The crime scene technicians lifted it from the door and photographed the shoeprint on the floor. They determined the shoe size to be a size 9 or 10.

Upstairs in the bedroom, no fingerprints were found. The safe was opened using technical drilling equipment, which went directly through the faceplate.

It seems that all four of the robberies occurred with an entry through the back door. Two were pried with a crowbar, and two were kicked in. No prints were found at the other robbery sites. What police are now looking for is a suspect who might be connected to these crimes. They know that all the robberies occurred late at night, and the same kinds of items were stolen from the house. The police began rounding up suspects.

List of Suspects

Suspect one: Glen Ferovski

He is a short, stocky Russian man who has just moved to the neighborhood. He works at the water treatment plant. He takes walks late at night because of his insomnia. He also spends a lot of time chopping wood in his backyard, which he sells for extra money. He also says that he was out driving around the night of the first two crimes; he could not sleep, so he drove around aimlessly. The other two nights, he claimed to have been sleeping. He also has a previous conviction for forging checks for large amounts of money. He wears a size 10 shoe.

Blood Typing   **77**

CRIME SCENE DO NOT CROSS CRIME SCENE DO NOT CROSS CRIME SCENE DO NOT CROSS CRIME SCENE DO NOT CROSS CRIME SCENE DO NOT CROSS CRIME SCENE DO NOT CROSS CRIME SCENE

Suspect two: Shelly Frazier

She is a kick boxer who grew up on the streets of New York. She moved to Nebraska two years ago to live with her sick aunt. Shelly is currently on probation for an assault that occurred in New York. She claims that it was self-defense, but the guy she beat up had five broken ribs, three broken fingers, and a broken leg. She is a fantastic kick boxer, the best in the state. She claims that she has not been home much, because she has been training for the national championship. She spends a lot of time in a cabin about twenty miles away, where she trains and focuses on the fight. She wears a $9\frac{1}{2}$ shoe.

Suspect three: Gustav Mariachi

He is a sixteen-year-old kid who is frequently suspended from school for fighting and insubordination. Because of the poor relationship he has with his parents, he often stays out all night. As of late, he has been spending more time away from home. He claims that he has a job with a guy who receives and ships merchandise. Apparently Gustav makes pretty good money, because he just bought expensive recording equipment for his guitar. He does not have any receipts, but police are working on tracing the serial numbers. The warehouse that he works out of mainly deals with opening crates with crowbars. Police are also keeping him under surveillance. He wears a size 10 shoe.

At the lab, scientists are working on the blood that was collected. The blood type will be determined and matched to one of the suspects, who have all given their blood samples.

First, students need to figure out the blood type of the sample taken from the crime scene. Prepare three separate samples. Then apply antiserum A and have students note the reaction. Does it clump? Now try antiserum B and repeat the process until finished. Students should be able to determine the blood type. Shelly Frazier should be the match, so make sure the test tubes correspond.

Now prepare samples 1, 2, and 3 on slides. Have students look at them under the microscope and record their observations.

Next, have them apply antiserum A to all three samples. Make note if any of them clump. Complete the same task again using antiserum B, and so forth. Through their observations, students should be able to match up to Shelly Frazier. You can change the suspect by matching samples before the lab starts.

Springboard to Writing

Allotted time: sixty minutes; three days for polished final draft

> *You are the expert lab technician for the local crime lab. You have been working on a high-profile case involving a murder. It was quite messy, so there was plenty of blood to test. You did find your tests conclusive and can say with a high degree of certainty that the DNA from the blood matches that of the suspect.*

78   *Partners in Crime*

CRIME SCENE DO NOT CROSS CRIME SCENE DO NOT CROSS CRIME SCENE DO NOT CROSS CRIME SCENE DO NOT CROSS CRIME SCENE DO NOT CROSS CRIME SCENE DO NOT CROSS CRIME SCENE

As the court date nears, you are subpoenaed to appear in court and give your testimony. The defense lawyer has a great track record for getting his clients off. You have to testify about the process of creating a DNA profile. Your testimony is highly important because most of the other evidence is circumstantial. The district attorney is depending on you to explain to the court exactly what you did and how you reached your conclusions. Your testimony could decide whether or not this man is convicted.

The trial begins and, as the expert, you take the stand. First, the lawyer asks you how blood is identified by type. Using the information learned from the lab, explain to the court how blood is typed. The DNA explanation will come later.

After the students have finished their rough draft, have them go back and circle the first word of every sentence. Students should make a list of all the words in a vertical row. Then they will be able to see how varied their sentence beginnings are. Tell them that within a paragraph the same word should not be used twice to start a sentence. Have students think about starting sentences with prepositional phrases, adverbial clauses, or even predicates. Once they begin doing this, they should also see that as the length of sentences begins varying, the flow of their paper is enhanced. You are looking for topic sentences, sequential order of facts, sentence structure, and key terms from the lab. This activity should take approximately one class period. Use the assessment for grading.

CSI Notebook

Allotted time: fifteen minutes
Think about the Case of the Foot. Have students recall the process of typing blood. Explain why it makes for good circumstantial evidence and not hard evidence. They should explain the difference between the two and why blood typing is considered circumstantial.

Assessment

- **Mastery (A).** Student has topic sentences in every paragraph. Student explains events in the correct order. Student has sentences that do not start with the same word more than twice. Student uses all terms from science lab.
- **Proficient (B).** Student has adequate topic sentences in every paragraph. Student explains events but could be more descriptive. Student starts sentences with the same word more than twice. Student uses adequate terms from the science lab.
- **Satisfactory (C).** Student does not start every paragraph with a topic sentence. Student does not explain process in order. Student starts sentences with the same word more than four times. Student uses limited words from the science lab.

Blood Typing   **79**

CRIME SCENE DO NOT CROSS CRIME SCENE DO NOT CROSS CRIME SCENE DO NOT CROSS CRIME SCENE DO NOT CROSS CRIME SCENE DO NOT CROSS CRIME SCENE DO NOT CROSS CRIME SCENE

- **Unsatisfactory (D).** Student does not have topic sentences. Student does not explain process. Student starts majority of sentences with the same word. Student uses minimal words from the science lab.
- **Insufficient (F).** Student writes a paper about the case that has nothing to do with blood typing.

Lesson Accommodations and Modifications

Students who are not proficient writers or are not sure how to start sentences with different words may have difficulty with this activity. Set a limit of four sentences starting with the same word. Provide a word bank for students to choose from when incorporating words from the lab. (This works for ESL students too.) There should be a topic sentence in every paragraph. They may also provide less detailed explanations of the process.

For Further Study

If students wish to find out more about blood typing, have them present a short history of the use of blood in crime scene investigation. Have them put together a time line on a poster board or using PowerPoint; they will get a better understanding of the progress blood has made throughout the years.

If a student is interested in blood typing as a career, he or she needs to follow the path of serology and genetics. The same guidelines as for a DNA specialist should be followed.

References

Butler, John. *Forensic DNA Typing: Biology and Technology Behind STR Markers.* Durham, N.C.: Academic Press, 2001.

Conklin, Barbara G., Gardner, Robert, and Shortelle, Dennis. *Encyclopedia of Forensic Science.* Phoenix: Oryx, 2002.

Evett, Ian, and Weir, Bruce. *Interpreting DNA Evidence: Statistical Genetics for Forensic Scientists.* Sunderland, Mass.: Sinauer Associates, 1998.

Inman, Keith, and Rudin, Norah. *Introduction to Forensic DNA Analysis.* New York: CRC Press, 1997.

Lee, Henry, and O'Neill, Thomas. *Cracking Cases: The Science of Solving Crimes.* New York: Prometheus, 2002.

Melaon, Clifford, Safferstein, Richard, and James, Richard. *Criminalistics.* Upper Saddle River, N.J.: Prentice Hall College Division, 1997.

Miller, Hugh. *What the Corpse Revealed: Murder and the Science of Forensic Detection.* New York: St. Martin's Press, 1999.

Nickell, John. *Crime Science: Methods of Forensic Detection.* Lexington: University Press of Kentucky, 1999.

Owen, David. *Hidden Evidence.* Richmond Hill, Ontario: Firefly Books, 2000.

Chapter Six

DNA

Overview for Teachers

This unit takes some time to explain. General knowledge is provided for the students to use in the classroom. More in-depth information is offered to you for a better understanding of DNA.

DNA is the building block of life. Every individual has a unique genetic code that sets the person apart from the rest. The only people who have the same DNA are identical twins. Relatives will have similar DNA, but it's not exactly the same.

There are two sources of DNA. One is nuclear DNA, which is found in the nucleus of the cell. This material determines what kind of physical characteristics people have. It is a half-and-half mixture of the mother and father, is found in the nucleus of every cell in the body, and remains the same forever. The other is mtDNA, which is located in the mitochondria of a cell. This is different from nuclear DNA. It is maternally inherited; therefore paternal DNA does not show up in mtDNA. During conception, the tail falls off the sperm, thus losing the mitochondrial DNA of the father. It is passed on from generation to generation. So your mtDNA is the same as your furthest-back great-grandmother.

A new system is being implemented to build a database of offenders according to their DNA. It is called CODIS, which stands for Combined DNA Index System. It works the same way that AFIS does for fingerprints.

This chapter should begin with a visit from a biologist. Contact a local pharmaceutical company, crime lab, or university that specializes in DNA. The biologist should discuss identifying unknown substances at a crime scene, which can sometimes be traced to DNA. The speaker should also discuss the role that DNA plays in investigating crime scenes and its use in indicting criminals.

There are a number of crime scene sources that can be used for DNA. Have students generate a list on the board (which should include most or all of the following):

Blood

Hair

Saliva

Skin

Fingernails

Human waste

Bones

82 *Partners in Crime*

CRIME SCENE DO NOT CROSS CRIME SCENE DO NOT CROSS CRIME SCENE DO NOT CROSS CRIME SCENE DO NOT CROSS CRIME SCENE DO NOT CROSS CRIME SCENE DO NOT CROSS CRIME SCENE DO NOT CROSS CRIME SCENE

Teeth

Hair shafts and roots

Semen

Cigarette butts

Postage stamps

Dandruff

Personal items such as gum, a toothbrush, or other means
of collecting bodily fluids

Replicating DNA

When samples of DNA are submitted to the lab, the forensic scientist is responsible for isolating the DNA for testing. In the past, the process of DNA testing took weeks; crime labs were backed up and cases began to stack up.

In 1980, the first type of marker used for DNA testing was RFLP, which stands for restriction fragment length polymorphism. A 50–500 nanogram (ng) sample was needed to perform the test, and the DNA had to be heavy in molecular weight and intact. It also used six areas of comparison that gave odds of one in one billion of a match. RFLP required a restriction enzyme digestion process in which the enzyme slides along the base pairs until it recognizes a specific pair. Then it stops and digests or cuts the DNA molecule at that particular area. This is called a restriction site. Sometimes it cuts at multiple areas, causing fragments of DNA. These fragments, or "digested DNA," are then loaded into an agarose gel and placed in an electrophoresis chamber. The chamber is hooked up to an electrical source. DNA is negatively charged, so it will work its way to the positive end of the chamber where the current is. The fragments are eventually transferred to a membrane made of nylon or similar material. Radioactive probes are then applied to the membrane. The excess is removed and the membrane is x-rayed. The result is a DNA pattern that can then be analyzed or interpreted.

The latest method used in the lab is PCR, which stands for polymerase chain reaction. It is much quicker and easier than RFLP, taking only a couple of days to complete. Only 0.1 to 1 ng is needed for testing, which means a blood drop the size of a pinhead can be used. The sample can be somewhat degraded yet still produce excellent results. The accuracy is much higher too: one in one billion to one in one trillion!

The premise of how PCR works is temperature. Scientists use a thermocycler because of its ability to heat and cool. First, the double helix has to be split; for this the DNA is heated to approximately 94 degrees Celsius. This causes splitting and exposes the bases. Next, the temperature is lowered to 54–60 degrees Celsius, where annealing takes place. This is when the polymerase is allowed to bind to the single strand of DNA. The polymerase becomes the "chief in charge," so to speak. It translates the next base located on the chain. Lastly, the temperature is raised to 70–72 degrees Celsius, where the polymerase picks out the complementary DNA bases and adds on to the DNA chain. When the process is finished, the DNA is replicated the

DNA **83**

CRIME SCENE DO NOT CROSS CRIME SCENE DO NOT CROSS CRIME SCENE DO NOT CROSS CRIME SCENE DO NOT CROSS CRIME SCENE DO NOT CROSS CRIME SCENE DO NOT CROSS CRIME SCENE

same as the original. The thermocycler runs through thirty-two cycles. The formula for PCR is two to the thirty-second power, which equals about 4.3 billion copies of DNA. Now there is enough DNA to test for everyone involved in the case. Defense lawyers will have some for their scientists to test as well as anyone else who needs to testify in the case.

There are many components to the process of identifying DNA. For further research, please see the reference section of this chapter.

If your school has the funding to purchase a thermocycler (a used one might be $1,000–$3,000; try contacting local labs to see if they would be willing to donate one), please encourage the purchase. Otherwise, you will have to prepare the materials.

Introduction to Subject Matter

(to be read to students)

DNA is a recent discovery in the realm of science. It is involved frequently in both convicting and exonerating suspects and prison inmates. It is a complex chain of directions for your entire body. The only people who have the same DNA are identical twins, though they do not have the same fingerprints. Through technology, DNA can be reproduced from a blood drop half the size of a pinhead. The human body has two types of DNA, nuclear and mitochondrial. Nuclear DNA is half from your mom and half from your dad. The mtDNA is from your mother only. It can be traced back thousands of years to your earliest ancestors.

Vocabulary

Annealing	The beginning translation of the DNA base
Blood typing	Reveals what kind of antigens are or are not present in the blood
CODIS	Combined DNA Index System
Digested DNA	Fragments of DNA that have been cut by enzymes
DNA	Deoxyribonucleic acid
Electrophoresis chamber	Electrically charged chamber in which DNA separates itself
Mitochondrial DNA	Represented as mtDNA, taken from the mitochondria in the cell; contains maternal DNA
Nuclear DNA	DNA taken from the nucleus of the cell; a fifty-fifty mix of maternal and paternal DNA
PCR	Polymerase chain reaction; a DNA replication system
Restriction site	The area where the DNA molecule is cut by the enzyme
RFLP	Restriction fragment length polymorphism; used for DNA replication

Lesson Objectives (with Standards Guide Words)

- Students will learn the definition of DNA and incorporate such distinctions into writing and analysis. (Guide words: definition, analysis, process, writing, comparison, contrast)
- Students will learn the types of DNA and where they are found in the body, and incorporate such distinctions into writing and analysis. (Same guide words as in preceding objective)
- Students will learn which bodily fluids contain DNA and incorporate this knowledge into writing and analysis. (Same guide words as in preceding objective)
- Students will learn how DNA is amplified by the processes of RFLP and PCR and incorporate this information into writing and analysis. (Same guide words as in preceding objective)

Lesson and Learning Activity

Time allotted: preparation, three or four hours; activity, two to three hours
Purchase a DNA kit from a science supply company. The kit should contain at least two kinds of DNA that have been cut with restriction enzymes. It should also contain the appropriate solutions, gels, and staining reagents. You should pour the gel and let it sit overnight in a refrigerated area. Remove two of the DNA samples from the kit. Label them suspect one (Stephen) and suspect two (George). Stephen is responsible for the murder, so make sure they match up in the experiment.

Note that if materials are not available, you can contact a crime lab or other labs that may be able to provide, or even donate, the supplies.

For this activity, certain materials are needed:

> George's and Stephen's DNA, cut with Eco R1 (provided in the kit)
>
> George's and Stephen's DNA, cut with Sma1 (in kit)
>
> Crime scene DNA, cut with Eco R1 and Sma1 (in kit)
>
> Micropipettes
>
> Electrophoresis buffer and chamber
>
> Agarose gel
>
> Methylene blue
>
> Aluminum pie plate
>
> DC power supply

For Love or Money

On November 15, two hunters discovered a body in the woods where they often go. The corpse was that of a twenty-year-old woman who had been reported missing for three days. She was wrapped in a blanket that was covered with blood. There was evidence of defense wounds on her hands. She died of multiple stab wounds to her stomach and chest. When the crime scene unit arrived, they put the body in a body bag and took it to the morgue for further investigation. They carefully wrapped the blanket and placed it in an evidence bag. While investigators combed the area, they found several empty beer cans that still had some backwash of beer. The investigators concluded that the beer cans had been left there recently because they were not dried out. They also found several cigarette butts next to the body. These items were collected, labeled, and sent to the lab for testing.

At the morgue, investigators cut out sections of the bloody blanket for analysis. They also scraped the underside of the victim's fingernails. This was also labeled and sent off to the lab.

Police think that her boyfriend, George, was responsible for the murder. He is now a prime suspect in the case. At the station, he agreed to provide blood samples and skin scrapings. The other suspect is the victim's brother, Stephen. He hated his sister and was angry with her because she inherited all of their parents' money. He had been overheard talking about how he was mad at his sister and wanted to "pay her back." He was also brought in to the station and volunteered to give samples of his blood for analysis. Both specimens were sent off to the lab for processing.

DNA Lab

Place students in groups of four. (If enough materials are not available, it will have to be done as a class experiment.) Try to match students who are not daily acquaintances of one another. You can have students choose numbers or whatever you find feasible. Each member of the group should be given a responsibility. When it comes time to pipetting, one student should do it; this keeps the results consistent, since pipetting is not as easy as it looks. You might want to give a short lesson on pipetting before students begin. This should take approximately ten minutes.

The process:

1. Place the agarose gel in its gel bed into the electrophoresis gel chamber.
2. Add enough electrophoresis buffer to the gel chamber to ensure that the gel is covered.
3. Using a clean pipette, place 5 microliters (μl) of George's DNA cut with Eco R1 into cell one in the agarose gel.
4. Using another clean pipette, place 5 μl of Stephen's DNA cut with Sma1 into cell two in the agarose gel.
5. With a clean pipette, place 5 μl of Stephen's DNA cut with Eco R1 into cell three in the gel.
6. Use another pipette to place 5 μl of Stephen's DNA cut with Sma1 into cell four in the gel.
7. Take a new pipette to place 5 μl of the crime scene DNA cut with Eco R1 into cell five in the gel.
8. Use another pipette to place 5 μl of the crime scene DNA cut with Sma1 into cell six in the gel.

86   *Partners in Crime*

CRIME SCENE DO NOT CROSS CRIME SCENE DO NOT CROSS CRIME SCENE DO NOT CROSS CRIME SCENE DO NOT CROSS CRIME SCENE DO NOT CROSS CRIME SCENE DO NOT CROSS CRIME SCENE

9. Place the top on the gel chamber and hook up the power supply. It should be set between 100 and 150 volts. Let it run for approximately thirty minutes or until the samples have almost crossed the gel.

10. Turn off the power and slide the gel bed onto an aluminum plate.

11. Cover the gel with methylene blue dye. Leave it in for approximately ten minutes or until blue bands appear on the gel.

12. Pour out the methylene blue into a bottle and rinse the gel in water several times.

13. Place the gel on the light box and compare the DNA from the crime scene to the other samples.

Springboard to Writing

Allotted time: fifty minutes; four days for polished final draft

Using the scenario on page 77 about the DNA expert in court, have students continue their explanation of how DNA is amplified and identified. Since there is more information here, the paper should be longer, at least three pages. Students should follow the steps involved in how DNA is amplified as well as in the correlation of results. Also continue emphasizing sentence structure. This is a good follow-up activity to check for understanding of what sentence structure really is. This should be a long-term assignment. Allow students at least four days to complete this writing piece. Use the assessment for grading.

CSI Notebook (Cumulative Mystery)

Allotted time: thirty minutes

Since no DNA evidence was found at the crime scene of Jackie Morrin's house, detectives are beginning to look at suspects. Have students think about motive, and make a prediction who they think is responsible for the murder. Have them write a paper of approximately twenty-five to thirty sentences.

Suspect one: Biff Hagan

He was Jackie's boyfriend for the last five years. He works as a lifeguard at the beach during the summer and is a full-time college student during the year. He is working on a degree in criminal justice. Jackie paid his bills and tuition with her inheritance money from her grandmother (which was in the area of $3 million).

It has been rumored that Biff was a lady's man and spent many nights at the local bar flirting with women while Jackie was working at the local shelter for homeless people. He has also been arrested for fighting and assault (see his rap sheet). He has a short fuse and sometimes blows up in a screaming and yelling rage.

Rap Sheet for Biff Hagan

Name: Biff Hagan

Address: 147 N. Walnut Ave, Stetson, PA 19394

Social Security no.: 456–34–9127

DOB: 1/24/80

Height: 5'9"

Weight: 185 lbs.

Eye color: blue

Hair color: blond

AKAs: Hags, Biffster

Date(s) of arrest: 5/7/02, 7/8/02, 7/20/02

Arresting department: Dauphin County

Charges: public drunkenness, assault with brass knuckles, disorderly conduct in a public place

Disposition: defendant was drunk with a BAC over 0.1 every time. On last arrest, defendant was aggressive with the arresting officer.

Fingerprint classifications: loops

FBI no.: ISDN 5933

SID [state identification] no.: 78245

OTN [offense tracking number]: 98HT73

Suspect two: Magnus Jameson

Magnus is the contractor in charge of building the new home. He is a tall blond from Sweden. Rumors have floated around town that Magnus and Jackie were having a secret affair. It was kept discreet because of Biff's temper; no one really knew about it until now. The police found out from the neighbor next door, who said she saw the two kissing on the back deck as the sun was setting one evening. Magnus is new to town, having been here about four years. His Swedish accent makes him even more attractive to the girls. As far as police know, he does not have any prior arrests or record. Apparently, Jackie still owed Magnus the rest of the payment for finishing the house. The bill totaled $50,000.

Suspect three: Clifford Morrin

Clifford is Jackie's brother. He is quite upset because he did not inherit any money from his grandmother. The one requirement that he had to meet was to be either in college or have a decent job. He was always jealous of Jackie; she got more attention than he did. She won the awards; she was in the paper for her athletic ability. He felt he could not compete with her, so he fell into a life of trouble. Another neighbor in the community said he had seen Cliff wandering around the neighborhood the day before the body was discovered. See his attached rap sheet.

Jackie was not a huge fan of the bank, so she kept her money in a safe at her house. She would pay for everything with cash or a cashier's check. The police report does not show any tampering with the safe. It was hidden behind a portrait of her grandmother that hung on the dining room wall. The safe area was dusted for prints, but nothing turned up.

Assessment

- **Mastery (A).** Student has topic sentences in every paragraph. Student explains events in the correct order. Student has sentences that do not start with the same word more than twice. Student uses DNA terms from science lab.
- **Proficient (B).** Student has adequate topic sentences in every paragraph. Student explains events but could be more descriptive. Student starts sentences with the same word more than twice. Student uses adequate DNA terms from the science lab.
- **Satisfactory (C).** Student does not start every paragraph with a topic sentence. Student does not explain process in order. Student starts sentences with the same word more than four times. Student uses limited DNA words from the science lab.
- **Unsatisfactory (D).** Student does not have topic sentences. Student does not explain process. Student starts majority of sentences with the same word. Student uses minimal DNA words from the science lab.
- **Insufficient (F).** Student writes a paper about the case that has nothing to do with DNA.

Rap Sheet for Clifford Morrin

Name: Clifford Morrin

Address: 886 Long Rifle Road, Stetson, PA 19394

Social Security no.: 556–12–3972

DOB: 8/3/78

Height: 6'0"

Weight: 225 lbs.

Eye color: brown

Hair color: black

AKAs: none

Date(s) of arrest: 2/5/03, 3/7/03

Arresting department: Dauphin County

Charges: two counts of domestic disturbance at the residence of Jackie Morrin

Disposition: mean and belligerent

Fingerprint classifications: loops

FBI no.: ISDN 6875

SID no.: 55724

OTN: 23JF66

90   *Partners in Crime*

CRIME SCENE DO NOT CROSS CRIME SCENE DO NOT CROSS CRIME SCENE DO NOT CROSS CRIME SCENE DO NOT CROSS CRIME SCENE DO NOT CROSS CRIME SCENE DO NOT CROSS CRIME SCENE

Lesson Accommodations and Modifications

For students who do not understand the process of DNA identification completely, provide study guides and handouts that they can use in writing their paper. Modifications can be made in the area of sentence structure and amount of detail provided.

ESL learners might have a difficult time completing this paper. Allow extra time and set up an appointment for the ESL teacher to come in for better explanation to students.

For Further Study

If students are interested in DNA, have them research the published literature online or in a local library. They might also consider setting up a working relationship with a local biologist who specializes in DNA. Scientists may be available in some communities; if not, students can go online to approach scientific companies for assistance.

An expert in DNA needs a B.S. in biology. Classes consist of molecular biology, genetics, cell biology, and application of cell functions within the body. Lab training is also necessary to learn the process involved with DNA.

References

Baden, Michael. *Dead Reckoning.* New York: Simon and Schuster, 2001.

Baden, Michael. *Unnatural Death: Confessions of a Medical Examiner.* New York: Ivy Books, 1989.

Butler, John. *Forensic DNA Typing: Biology and Technology Behind STR Markers.* Durham, N.C.: Academic Press, 2001.

Conklin, Barbara G., Gardner, Robert, and Shortelle, Dennis. *Encyclopedia of Forensic Science.* Phoenix: Oryx, 2002.

Dix, Jay. *Time of Death, Decomposition, and Identification.* New York: CRC Press, 2000.

Evett, Ian, and Weir, Bruce. *Interpreting DNA Evidence: Statistical Genetics for Forensic Scientists.* Sunderland, Mass.: Sinauer Associates, 1998.

Inman, Keith, and Rudin, Norah. *Introduction to Forensic DNA Analysis.* New York: CRC Press, 1997.

Lee, Henry, and O'Neill, Thomas. *Cracking Cases: The Science of Solving Crimes.* New York: Prometheus, 2002.

Manhein, Mary. *The Bone Lady: Life as a Forensic Anthropologist.* New York: Penguin Books, 2000.

Melaon, Clifford, Safferstein, Richard, and James, Richard. *Criminalistics.* Upper Saddle River, N.J.: Prentice Hall College Division, 1997.

Miller, Hugh. *What the Corpse Revealed: Murder and the Science of Forensic Detection.* New York: St. Martin's Press, 1999.

Nickell, John. *Crime Science: Methods of Forensic Detection.* Lexington: University Press of Kentucky, 1999.

Owen, David. *Hidden Evidence.* Richmond Hill, Ontario: Firefly Books, 2000.

Spitz, Werner. *Spitz and Fisher Medico-Legal Investigation of Death* (3rd ed.). Springfield, Ill.: Charles C. Thomas, 1993.

Chapter Seven

Toxicology

Overview for Teachers

Toxicology is the study of the nature, effects, and detection of poisons and the treatment of poison. Crime labs of today have a toxicology section dealing with identifying substances in all parts of the human body and everyday products.

One of the major tools of the toxicologist is the mass spectrometer. This laboratory instrument measures the mass-to-charge ratio of individual molecules that have been converted into ions. The information is then used to determine the masses of the molecules. All elements have specific molecules that show on the mass spectrometer.

In the lab, scientists take a sample and run it through the mass spectrometer. It is then compared with a database of tens of thousands of chemicals and elements.

Unidentified substances are found in many places. They are most common when a person is caught with an unknown substance, liquid, or solid. Most of the time they are drugs. Police have special kits that can test the substance on the spot. These tests are packets that contain ampoules, activated by crushing. A sample of the suspect drug is placed inside and shaken up. Resulting colors tell whether or not the substance tests positive for a certain drug. However, it must also be sent to a lab for further testing to confirm the drug. The lab expert must first determine the characteristics of the substance and use it to test other substances. The expert should conduct more than one test to positively identify the substance; for best results, there should be several tests for identification. This requires adding chemicals and checking the reaction for color and odor. Another test is to place it on a hot plate to see what kind of reaction is generated.

In the case of poisoning, samples are needed from the autopsy. Blood, tissues, and sections of organs are most commonly used to perform toxicology tests. These tests reveal if any chemical has been ingested or otherwise taken into the body. (Incidentally, most women who murder their spouses choose poisoning as their weapon of choice.)

Water contamination is a part of toxicology. In this chapter, there is a groundwater contamination lab activity. This fits in perfectly with units on pH level and using universal indicators (pH stands for the power of hydrogen; this means how many hydrogen ions are in a liquid solution, which is what is actually being measured.)

Many people rely on groundwater for their drinking supply. It may have to travel a long distance to reach its destination, where it is purified. Some people have the luxury of artesian wells, which supply water from a well instead of the pipes used with groundwater. Sometimes there is a contamination of the drinking water. Factories and other establishments along the banks of a major waterway may dump things in the water that are not too healthy for the people drinking it. Toxins ranging from pesticides to fecal matter can be found in water.

Some people think that drinking from a stream in the woods is the freshest source of water. Well, think again. As animals cross the stream bed, they sometimes urinate or defecate in the water. If ingested, this could cause an experience known as CED (chronic explosive diarrhea). Also, when living things die in a stream, their decomposing tissues and matter float downstream. Tell students they shouldn't drink from any water source that has not been treated thoroughly.

In most labs, the mass spectrometer is coupled with chromatography, in the form of gas, liquid, and the newly discovered substance of plasma helping separate compounds before they are broken up into molecules.

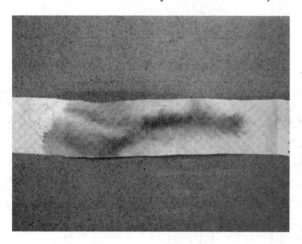

Chromatography is used to identify substances too. It separates and identifies individual chemical compounds in a solution or gas. It was first used in 1906 by a Russian named Mikhail Tsvet to separate plant pigments.

Basically, chromatography works in two stages. The first is stationary, in which the material absorbs the components of the mixture. The second phase is mobile, in which the components become soluble. Components are absorbed at different rates; hence they separate in the process. Chromatography can be used with paper, thin layer glass plates, liquid, and gas. It may be used to identify a certain ink or even a lipstick. Lab experts use it to help them match substances that have been collected. In this chapter, ink is used as an illustration of chromatography (see the figure). It can be easily identified by conducting simple experiments using coffee filter paper.

Introduction to Subject Matter

(to be read to students)
Toxicology involves the study of chemistry and how it affects environments and living organisms. Chemicals can enter the body in several ways. They can be ingested, which means that something poisonous is swallowed. They can be inhaled when fumes or gases are present. They can also get into your body if something toxic contacts your skin or gets into your eyes. Toxicology also deals with breaking material into its basic components. With the technology available today, a paint chip or shard of glass can be analyzed and broken down into its various chemical makeups.

Vocabulary

Ampoule packet	A small sealed glass container that holds a measured amount of reagent to react with specific known illegal drugs
Artesian well	A natural water supply that can be tapped as a water source
Atomic mass	A unit of measurement that weighs the amount of atoms in an element
Autopsy	The medical examination of a dead body in order to establish the cause and circumstances of death
Charge	A fundamental characteristic of matter, responsible for all electric and electromotive forces, expressed in two forms known as positive and negative
Chromatography	A method of finding out which components a gaseous or liquid mixture contains; involves passing it through or over something that absorbs components at different rates
Ions	An atom or group of atoms that have acquired an electric charge by losing or gaining one or more electrons
Mass spectrometer	An instrument used to separate compounds and measure their molecular weight
Mobile phase	Components become soluble and travel, leaving marks of separation
Molecule	The smallest physical unit of a substance that can exist independently, consisting of one or more atoms held together by chemical forces
Pesticide	A chemical substance used to kill pests, especially insects
pH	Measure of the number of hydrogen ions in a liquid solution
Stationary phase	The absorption of material into chromatography paper
Toxicology	The study of the nature, effects, and detection of any element that has a toxic effect

Lesson Objectives (with Standards Guide Words)

- Students will understand the term *toxicology* and illustrate examples. (Guide word: definition)
- Students will learn the term *pH*. (Guide word: definition)
- Students will learn to measure pH with a universal indicator and illustrate examples. (Guide words: process learning, constructivist, measurement, definition)
- Students will learn what a mass spectrometer is and illustrate an example. (Same guide words as preceding objective)

94   *Partners in Crime*

CRIME SCENE DO NOT CROSS CRIME SCENE DO NOT CROSS CRIME SCENE DO NOT CROSS CRIME SCENE DO NOT CROSS CRIME SCENE DO NOT CROSS CRIME SCENE DO NOT CROSS CRIME SCENE

- Students will learn the meaning of chromatography and illustrate examples. (Same guide words)

- Students will learn how chromatography is used to solve crimes and illustrate examples. (Same guide words)

- Students will learn how to conduct a chromatography test on a sample and illustrate examples. (Same guide words)

- Students will differentiate between stationary and mobile phase and illustrate examples. (Same guide words, plus: comparison, contrast)

Lessons and Learning Activities

Allotted time: preparation one hour, class two days

Part One: Scenario

For the teacher: You will need a sample test tube for each group. Fill the test tube with 10 ml of water. Test the water beforehand to find out the pH level. If it has a blue color, the pH is around 7. You can leave the water as is or add chemicals to raise or lower the pH to 7.

Other materials:

Dropper

Chemplates

Universal indicator

The Pocono Pond Mystery

On June 3, 2004, Mr. Hutchins shows up at the township building demanding to speak to a supervisor. The secretary asks him to have a seat while she goes to get Miss Davis. After ten minutes, Davis appears and asks Hutchins if she can help him.

In an irate voice, he explains that his two dogs have become very sick in the past day. He thinks that someone has polluted the water with pesticides. According to Hutchins, the water is the only possible reason for the dogs getting sick. He takes them there to go swimming. They love the water, and it's good practice for duck season.

Hutchins is quite concerned about his two dogs. They are his only friends because he has never married. Hutchins demands that Davis find out what is wrong with the water—and if anything happens to his dogs, he will sue the township. Davis thanks him for his time and says she will get back to him as soon as possible. She returns to her office and starts making phone calls. The first person she calls is Joe Kane, who is in charge of the hazmat team for the county.

Joe goes to the pond and does a sample water test. As he mixes in the chemicals, he discovers that it is contaminated with some kind of toxin found in pesticides. He knows for sure because the chemical reaction shows a red color, which means the water has a very low pH. Also, when

Toxicology

95

CRIME SCENE DO NOT CROSS CRIME SCENE DO NOT CROSS CRIME SCENE DO NOT CROSS CRIME SCENE DO NOT CROSS CRIME SCENE DO NOT CROSS CRIME SCENE DO NOT CROSS CRIME SCENE

he adds a reagent, it turns the water to greenish blue, indicating that a pesticide is present. He goes back to the township to look at a map of the area.

He remembers that a week ago, there was a truck spill on Route 95. The township brought in the hazmat team for a safe cleanup. The Pocono Creek does run underneath the highway, but it is believed nothing leaked into the water from the spill. He decides to run a test anyway just to make sure.

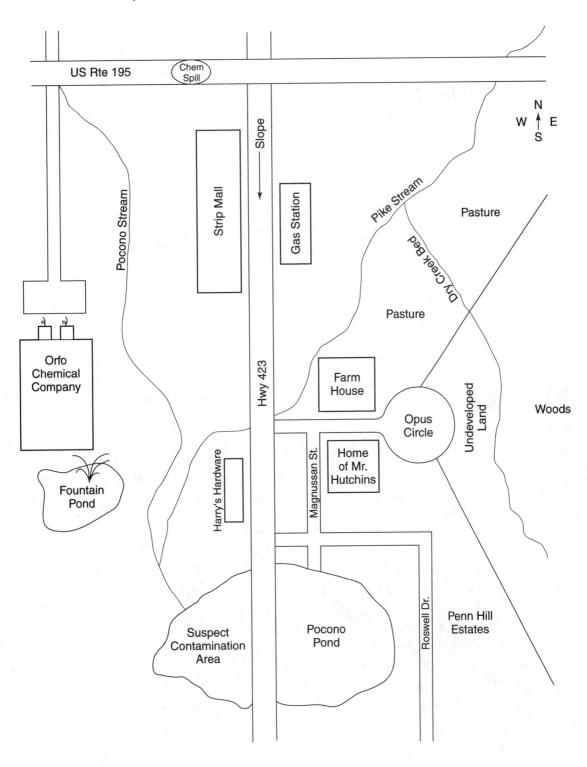

96   *Partners in Crime*

CRIME SCENE DO NOT CROSS CRIME SCENE DO NOT CROSS CRIME SCENE DO NOT CROSS CRIME SCENE DO NOT CROSS CRIME SCENE DO NOT CROSS CRIME SCENE DO NOT CROSS CRIME SCENE

As the teacher, you need a sample test tube for each group. Follow the instructions appearing in the earlier list of materials.

Have students use a dropper to place five drops in three of the chemplates. Then have them put in two drops of universal indicator. This changes the color of the water to reveal the pH level. The outcome should be a blue color, which shows a pH of 7. Although testing for pH, tell students that these particular pesticides have a low pH level. Once they find an area with this low pH level, they can test for the pesticide. Students should record their results on their map, indicating the color and pH level of the test done at a particular location.

Part Two: Lab

Review the results from the first test. Discuss the conclusions with the class to see if they have any other ideas. Use the map as a guide. When a student mentions the Orfo Chemical Company, tell students that it is the next test site. Take them back to the scenario.

> *Next, Joe notices that Orfo Chemicals has a plant on the Pocono Creek too. They use the water for making chemicals. They have strict guidelines to follow and are supposed to test every month. Joe thinks this is his best bet, so he heads there to test the water.*

Again, create two sample test tubes for each group and have the students follow the same procedures to add drops, label tests, and so on.

Make sure that students label their tests above and downstream from the plant. They should record their results on their map.

Discuss the results with the class and ask them where they should look next. A student should come up with the answer to test the pond, to be really sure the water is polluted. Then go back to the scenario.

Part Three

> *Joe is quite surprised that he has not found anything by the plant. They have been cited in the past for polluting the water with high levels of toxins. Joe wants to make sure that the pond is really contaminated, so he goes to Pocono Pond to test the water.*

For the teacher:
Make a sample test tube for each group with 10 ml of water.

Mix some lemon juice, vinegar, or any acidic solution to bring the pH level to about 2. Students should follow the same process for testing using the chemplates. Once they find out that they have a high pH level, ask them to use the reagent for pesticide testing. For this, you should mix a 10 ml solution with some baking soda or ammonia. Have students add two drops of the solution to the chemplate. If the solution is strong enough, it should bring the color to a bluish green. Tell students that this is a positive test for pesticides in the water. Students should document their findings on their map.

Toxicology **97**

CRIME SCENE DO NOT CROSS CRIME SCENE DO NOT CROSS CRIME SCENE DO NOT CROSS CRIME SCENE DO NOT CROSS CRIME SCENE DO NOT CROSS CRIME SCENE DO NOT CROSS CRIME SCENE

Now that the students know the pond is definitely contaminated, have them generate ideas of what should be done next. Then take them back to the scenario.

Part Four

At 11:00 the next morning, Davis gets a phone call from Hutchins. His dogs were at the veterinary hospital all night. He has just received word that they have both died. Infuriated, he is now planning on suing the township for the loss of his dogs. In a panic, Davis assures Hutchins that they will find out who is responsible and bring them to justice.

After that, she calls Joe to find out how he is doing. Joe reports that the pond is definitely contaminated with some sort of pesticide. He has not completed all of his tests yet. Now the question is, What part of the stream is being dumped in? He has one more area to test. He knows that a farmer named Hendricks uses pesticides to treat his corn crops. He is almost certain that this is the source. Without further delay, he heads up to the Hendricks farm house. He explains to Hendricks what he is doing and asks if he can test the water on his property. The farmer agrees and lets Joe get to work. Joe decides to test upstream and downstream from the crop area.

For the teacher:
Repeat the procedure of creating sample test tubes for each group. When students put in two drops of universal indicator, it will change the color of the water to show the pH level. The outcome should be blue, which shows a pH of 7.

By a process of elimination, students will find that the last place that has not been tested is Harry's Hardware. Take them back to the scenario.

Part Five

Scratching his head, Joe is extremely confused. The only place left along the creek is Harry's Hardware. Joe pulls up to the hardware store to speak to Harry. His son tells Joe that he is out back cleaning out some cans. As Joe walks around back, he sees Harry rinsing out some containers in the stream. In an instant, Joe knows exactly what is happening. Harry is cleaning out the containers with bug pesticide in them! As Joe approaches, Harry stops to talk to Joe. Being the old man he is, he does not realize what he is doing. Joe takes a test kit and samples the water. What do you think happens?

For the teacher:
Repeat the test tube work with universal indicator. Blue shows a pH of 7.

Joe has no clue what is going on. He heads back down to the pond to survey the area. He ends up where the mouth of the creek feeds into the pond. Off to the side in the bushes, Joe notices a large white bucket sitting at the edge of the woods, half shrouded with twigs and leaves. Curious, he walks over to the container and finds out it is (or was) filled with a high

98   *Partners in Crime*

CRIME SCENE DO NOT CROSS CRIME SCENE DO NOT CROSS CRIME SCENE DO NOT CROSS CRIME SCENE DO NOT CROSS CRIME SCENE DO NOT CROSS CRIME SCENE DO NOT CROSS CRIME SCENE

concentration of pesticide that was to be diluted with water. He immediately gets on the phone and calls Davis. She sends the police over to take it in as evidence and have it tested at the lab.

At the lab, scientists have enough material to do a test.

For the teacher:

Repeat the sampling with lemon juice, vinegar, or an acidic solution and then baking soda or ammonia (see the earlier instructions).

Now that the students have found a container matching the sample from the pond, they should be able to deduce that Hutchins dumped it in there himself so that he could sue the township for money. How would the police know that someone dumped a pesticide in the pond?

Well, he has threatened to sue the township, so as the teacher you can take it a step further and plant fingerprints on the bucket. Match them to Hutchins. It also turns out that after detectives looked further they find a record on his credit card indicating he bought the pesticide the day before at Harry's Hardware.

Chromatography Activity

Allotted time: fifty minutes

Who Wrote the Note?

The president of a large corporation received a note from someone that they were planning to sabotage the company's name by publishing a negative letter in the Wall Street Journal. *The president was very upset. She noticed that the handwriting looked familiar. Three secretaries worked for her at desks on the same floor.*

One was named Laurie Nebbia. She had a great personality and was a fantastic worker. She sometimes stayed late to finish her work.

Next was Cathie White. She was very humorous and kept the president in high spirits. She had been known to fly off the handle sometimes and rant and rave at people.

Last was Pam Gerhart. She was a sweet young woman who was polite and helpful and never said more than she had to.

The president suspected all three of them because they were over-worked and underpaid. Despite her dubious efforts of arguing with her colleagues, she could not obtain a raise for them.

Police collected felt tip pens with blue ink from each secretary's desk. They were sent to the lab along with the note. The lab experts ran a test on the ink used in the note and on the pens collected. Each secretary had three blue pens. All nine samples were grouped according to the secretary. When detectives interviewed the three suspects, they all denied they were involved.

All of them provided a handwriting sample that was also sent to the lab to be viewed by a handwriting expert. However, two nights later, the lab was burglarized, and the note and handwriting samples went missing. Since the lab technician had already run a test on the ink used in the letter, she could still test the other inks to determine whose desk the pen came from.

This activity should take approximately one class period. You need:

Three large beakers

Straight piece of wire (a coat hanger will work) approximately six inches in length

Paper clips

Hole puncher

Water

Coffee filters cut into strips about four inches long

Nine pens with blue ink

Directions for students:

1. Cut the filter paper into strips about four inches long. You should have nine pieces all together. Fold one end of the strip into a point.

2. Place a paper clip at the pointed end of each filter paper. This will keep the filter paper from curling.

3. Punch a hole in the other end of each filter paper.

4. Using one of the pens, place a sample mark (a dot) just above the paper clip.

5. Thread a piece of wire through the end of the filters where the holes have been punched. Make sure they do not touch each other. There should be three strips of filter paper on each wire.

6. Place each strand of wire over each beaker so the nine pieces of filter paper are suspended inside the beakers.

7. Carefully add water to the beaker until it reaches the point of covering the paper clips and the pointed ends of the nine filter papers. Do not cover the ink marks in the water.

8. Let everything sit until the water has dampened most of the length (two-thirds to three-fourths) of the strips.

9. Remove each piece of wire from the beaker and let it sit on a paper towel until it dries.

10. Once it dries, you will have completed the chromatography process.

Have students compare marks on the filter paper with the sample taken from the note. The students should be able to match up the ink with the sample. The sample should match with Cathie White.

Springboard to Writing

Allotted time: two days; four days for polished final draft
This story is to be read to the students (or it can be received as a handout).

The Sloppy Kisser

On Tuesday, April 20, 2004, Jamal Windle received a mysterious love letter in his mailbox. On the front of it was his name written in green marker. On the back, the envelope was sealed and had a sloppy, smudgy lip imprint. Jamal thought it was obviously a letter from his new girlfriend, Josephine. But when he opened the letter, he found a threatening note: "If you love me, then you should be ready to die for me."

Jamal had never received a letter like that before. Being the jolly fellow he is, he was rather shaken up and a little scared. Could Josephine be responsible for this? She was a sweetheart. Jamal, who is a forensic scientist, decided to get to the bottom of this. He had to figure out a way to get into Josephine's makeup kit and check out her lipsticks. If he got a sample from her, then he could do a chromatography test on them and find out for sure. Now the question is, how will he do it?

Your job is to write a descriptive essay from Jamal's point of view. In your essay, explain how you will obtain the lipsticks from her makeup bag. Then explain how you will test the lipsticks to see if they match up. Here is how you will be graded.

We will use two model essays that you will read through and grade as a class. Notice differences between the two so that we can generate a list of them on the board. These should be taken into consideration when you write your paper.

(To the teacher: use the assessment grading.)

Sample Essay One

Lukas Hendrix, Period 2, "Lopsided Lipstick"

My name is Jamal and I want to tell you about this crazy letter I got. It had a big kiss on the back of it and it said that I was going to die. I didn't really believe it at first, but then I thought it might be my girlfriend. She is real nice and I think she is cool. Why would she do something like this to me?

The first thing I did was take a sample of the lipstick that was used on the back of the letter. I put it on some paper and let it sit in water for a few minutes. Then after it dried, it had all these neat colors on it. This is called chromatography. I do this at my work all the time. Now that I had a sample of the lipstick, I had to find out if it was from my girlfriend Josephine. I needed a plan to get into her house and get her lipstick.

I called her on Friday night when I got home from work. I asked her if I could bring over some popcorn and a movie to watch. She thought about it and decided it would be a great idea. She wanted me to rent a scary movie. I thought this was weird because she doesn't like that kind of stuff. I agreed and hung up the phone.

At the store I picked up *Psycho on the Loose.* It was a movie about a psycho that escapes and runs around killing people. I also bought some popcorn for us. Then I headed to Josephine's house.

When I got there, she had all of the lights turned off and candles were lit all over the place. She welcomed me in and asked me to get comfortable. We popped in the movie and began to watch the previews. This is when I decided to make my move. I told her I had to go to the bathroom before the movie started. When I got into the bathroom I locked the door behind me. I found her makeup bag under the sink. I took all of the lipstick that was in there and shoved them in my pocket. I flushed the toilet and came back to the living room. I told Josephine that I forgot to feed my dog and had to run home quick and I would be back in a half an hour. She agreed and let me go. I thought she could tell I was lying, but I got away with it.

When I got home, I set up my chromatography experiment. I tested all of the lipsticks. When I finally got to the last one, it was a match. I couldn't believe she wanted to kill me. I called the cops and told them what happened. They came to my house first, where I showed them my experiments that I did. Then they went to her house and arrested her for attempted murder. Wow! That was a close one.

Sample Essay Two

Marshall Clapton, Period 3, "The Case of Josephine's Joke"
On Friday morning I received a note in my red mailbox at the end of my driveway. Inside the box were regular bills and weekly flyers. As I stumbled across this odd note, it occurred to me that it only had my name on it and a kiss on the back. The writing was in what appeared to be a green marker. The kiss on the back was smudged and rather sloppy. I haven't received a note like this since I was in seventh grade. I was a little skeptical, but I opened it anyway. Inside, it said, "If you love me, then you should be ready to die for me." I was quite shocked because you never know what kind of whackos are out there. Then a sudden thought hit me like a Mack truck; Josephine! She was my new girlfriend. We had been dating for about two weeks now. She has been talking about getting more serious lately. I don't know if I can make that decision just yet. Anyhow, I took the note inside and locked the door behind me. I sat down at the kitchen table eating my breakfast of poached eggs and crispy bacon. Along with a steamy cup of coffee, I was ready to think about this.

I didn't really know Josephine that well, so I decided that since I am a forensic scientist I could figure out if she was really the one responsible for the note. I didn't want to call the police yet because it could all be a joke. After I gobbled down my breakfast and sipped my coffee, I left for work along with the strange note.

At work, I have all of the necessary equipment to perform chromatography experiments. I collected a sample from the envelope using a clean swab. Then I took a piece of chromatography paper which is about two inches wide by four inches long. Using the lipstick-covered swab, I made a blot about one inch above the bottom of the paper. Then I filled a beaker with 75 milliliters of acetone. Using a hole puncher, I punched a hole in the top of the paper. I placed a medium-sized metal wire through the hole to suspend the paper above the acetone. The paper rested in the solution about a half an inch deep. After about five minutes, the color had slowly worked its way up the paper. I took it out of the solution and laid it down to dry. After another ten minutes, I had a beautiful stream of colors climbing up the chromatography paper. Now that I had a sample, I would have to figure out a way to test some lipstick at Josephine's house.

I called her during lunch and asked if I could come over later and cook a delicious lobster dinner for her. She said that would be fantastic. Lobster was her favorite and she thought my cooking was to die for. As I hung up the phone, she said that she loved me. I responded with "I have to go now and I will see you tonight."

Now I had to decide what to make for dinner and how to get into her bathroom to test her lipstick.

Before I left for Josephine's house, I placed some coffee filter paper in my pocket. It serves the same purpose as chromatography paper. I jumped into my sporty red Porsche and zipped over to her house.

When I got there, she had some light jazz playing on the stereo and the table was set for two with candlelight. I must say that it did look most delightful. She offered me a Coke while I was preparing our meal. As I was chopping the onions for our scalloped potato mix, I "accidentally" cut my finger. As Josephine screamed, I told her that I could take care of this if I could just use her bathroom. I wrapped a kitchen towel around my finger and went to the bathroom. Luckily for me, she did not like the sight of blood and stayed in the kitchen to finish our dinner.

When I got into the bathroom, I searched frantically for her makeup bag. I finally found it under the sink next to her curling iron and hair dryer. I quickly pulled out my filter paper and began to work. I pulled up the stopper in the sink and poured her nail polish remover in there. It is made of acetone. I found three different kinds of lipstick in the case. One was a red Max Factor. The other two were L'Oreal red lipstick with extra shine. I rubbed a little dot on each piece of paper like I did at the lab. I held them in the sink for one minute. The filter paper seemed to absorb the acetone faster, so I did not have to keep it in there as long. I turned the water back on again as I heard a knock that startled me enough to bang my knee on the sink. Josephine asked if I was all right. "Fine," I said in a strained voice. "The bleeding has almost stopped. Just a few more minutes and I will be as good as new."

With that she left. The paper was starting to dry. I remembered that I had brought the sample with me from the lab. I pulled it out of my pocket for comparison. It looked like the Max Factor lipstick was going to match! One minute later and the process was complete. It was a perfect match.

I panicked and looked around for an escape route. Lucky for me she lived on the first floor and there was a window big enough for me to fit through—or so I thought. About halfway through, my shirt got caught on a nail on the windowsill. There was another knock on the door. I screamed and wiggled as hard as I could.

"RRRRIIPPPPPP!!" went my brand new Polo shirt. I had spent $90 on that shirt too. Oh well, I ran down the street half-naked until I reached an old phone booth at the corner. It was littered with graffiti and cigarette butts. I put in my quarter and dialed 911. I told the police of my amazing adventure and they were stunned that someone other than themselves could solve a crime. They responded immediately, arrested Josephine, and my life was spared.

Now I have to go to psychotherapy because I can't date women who wear lipstick!

Assessment

- **Mastery (A).** Student has a specific order and transitions from one idea to the next. Student uses elaborate details. Student writing is appropriate for audience.
- **Proficient (B).** Student has adequate order and transitions from one idea to the next. Student uses adequate detail. Student writing is acceptable for audience.
- **Satisfactory (C).** Student has limited order and transitions are limited. Student uses limited detail. Student writing is not necessarily geared toward intended audience.
- **Unsatisfactory (D).** Student has events out of order and transitions are choppy. Student uses minimal detail. Student writing is hard to understand because of mistakes.
- **Insufficient (F).** Student does not write about the topic. Sentences are incoherent and paper cannot be understood.

Lesson Accommodations and Modifications

Students who do not understand how to correctly score and revise a paper might have trouble with this assignment. Have them use the first essay as a starting point and rewrite it so it sounds better. This way they have the writing in front of them and do not have to create a new paper. This works well for ESL students too. It allows them to take language already written and make it better, which can be done under the direct instruction of the ESL teacher.

CSI Notebook

Allotted time: fifteen minutes
Have students think about the importance of the periodic chart. What if we did not have certain elements such as carbon or nitrogen? Have them generate a list of elements that they think are most important to our survival. They should write a sentence or two explaining why these elements are needed for us to survive.

For Further Study

If students are interested in learning more about chromatography, they can find various resources online. They can also perform chromatography tests at home. They can test various products in their house using beauty products such as lipstick and nail polish. Markers and pens work well too. Nail polish remover can serve as a mobile phase, or water in the case of water-soluble products. Students can present their chromatography results by photographing them or bringing in the actual results from the experiments.

If a person is interested in becoming a forensic toxicologist or chemist, he or she needs a bachelor's degree in chemistry, toxicology, pharmacology, chemical engineering, physics, or some other related field. From there, on-the-job training and experience in the lab will be useful.

104   *Partners in Crime*

CRIME SCENE DO NOT CROSS CRIME SCENE DO NOT CROSS CRIME SCENE DO NOT CROSS CRIME SCENE DO NOT CROSS CRIME SCENE DO NOT CROSS CRIME SCENE DO NOT CROSS CRIME SCENE

Cumulative Mystery

Allotted time: fifty minutes

After detectives finished dusting for fingerprints, one of the detectives went to throw away her gloves in the trash can. There in the trash can she noticed a crumpled-up piece of paper. She asked one of the detectives who still had his gloves on to come over and retrieve it from the trash. He did and he opened the crinkled paper to see a note that said, "I hate you and you will never get away with this. I am watching you, Jackie." It was written in black ink. It looked as though it were done with a marker rather than a pen. Following procedure, the detective photographed the note and packaged it to be sent to the lab. Detectives would need a warrant to search the houses and cars of the suspects to see if they could find a match.

You can use the same activity as in the lesson and learning activity. Just substitute the three names with the three suspects in this case. The ink will match with a pen found in Jackie's house.

References

Ardery, Robert. *Liquid Chromatography, Mass Spectrometry: An Introduction.* Hoboken, N.J.: Wiley, 2003.

Baselt, Randall. *Disposition of Toxic Drugs and Chemicals in Man.* Foster City, Calif.: Chemical Toxicology Institute, 2002.

Casarett, Louis. *Casarett and Doull's Toxicology: The Basic Science of Poisons.* Upper Saddle River, N.J.: Prentice Hall, 1986.

Conklin, Barbara G., Gardner, Robert, and Shortelle, Dennis. *Encyclopedia of Forensic Science.* Phoenix: Oryx, 2002.

Ferner, R. E., and Norman, Elizabeth. *Forensic Pharmacology: Medicines, Mayhem, and Malpractice.* New York: Oxford University Press, 1996.

Hoffman, Edmond, and Stroobant, Vincent. *Mass Spectrometry: Principles and Applications.* Hoboken, N.J.: Wiley, 2003.

Levine, Barry. *Principles of Forensic Toxicology.* Washington, D.C.: AACC Press, 2003.

McLafferty, Fred. *Interpretation of Mass Spectra* (4th ed.). Herndon, Va.: University Science Books, 1996.

Nickell, John. *Crime Science: Methods of Forensic Detection.* Lexington: University Press of Kentucky, 1999.

Owen, David. *Hidden Evidence.* Richmond Hill, Ontario: Firefly Books, 2000.

Trimbell, John. *Introduction to Toxicology* (3rd ed.). New York: Taylor and Francis, 2001.

Williams, Robert James. *The Principles of Toxicology: Environmental and Industrial Applications* (2nd ed.). Hoboken, N.J.: Wiley Interscience, 2000.

Zonderman, John. *Beyond the Crime Lab.* Hoboken, N.J.: Wiley, 1999.

Chapter Eight

Microbes and Drowning Victims

Overview for Teachers

This chapter should begin with a visit from a forensic biologist, a person who specializes in small organisms that are of value to a criminal investigation. A biologist can be found at a local university, or a pharmaceutical company. Water contains certain microbes and diatoms, which may be used to identify a victim who was drowned and then later removed. A sample of water must be extracted from the lungs as well as the source of water.

For background information, students should be familiar with the various types of microbes and diatoms. Some common ones are Spirogyra, Cladophora, Euglena, Phacus, Synedra, and Ulothrix. (See figures on page 106.) These can be found in water samples everywhere. Try some water sources and see if they are present. If not, you can easily grow them by placing some algae in water and letting it sit for a week.

When someone drowns, the lungs fill up with water and prevent any air from coming in. As the lungs fill up, a phenomenon called pulmonary edema occurs as water is rapidly taken into the bloodstream and a violent increase in blood flow is sent to the heart. This in turn creates a white froth that exudes from the mouth and nose.

Another indication of a drowning is a cadaveric spasm. This occurs when the victim grabs onto something to assist in getting to the top for air. The corpse assumes the position of someone getting ready to complete a bench press.

There are other medical factors associated with drowning, but they vary with the victim.

In the case of a drowning, the investigator must first locate the body. This is done with certified divers who use a lifeline rope and perform a line search. That means they form a line of divers and search the bottom of the suspected area looking for the victim.

Once the victim is found, the body must be retrieved and brought to shore. This is a delicate process because water can wash away evidence left by the perpetrator. After the body is brought to shore, it is immediately laid out on a body bag to ensure the integrity of any evidence that may still be on the body, and to keep any other contamination on the ground from getting onto the body.

106 **Partners in Crime**

CRIME SCENE DO NOT CROSS CRIME SCENE DO NOT CROSS CRIME SCENE DO NOT CROSS CRIME SCENE DO NOT CROSS CRIME SCENE DO NOT CROSS CRIME SCENE DO NOT CROSS CRIME SCENE

Spirogyra

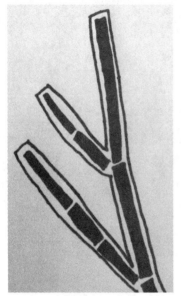

Cladophora

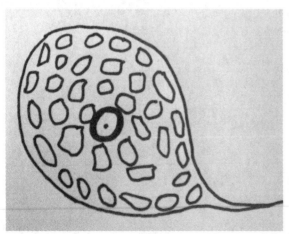

Euglena

Phacus

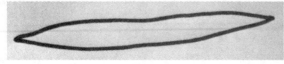

Synedra

Ulothrix

Water slows the decomposition process of a body. One week above ground is equal to two weeks underwater, which is equal to eight weeks underground. Sometimes investigators can make an educated guess as to how long the body has been submersed by the condition of the body.

In some instances, saponification occurs. This is when the adipose tissue (fat tissue) is converted into a soap or waxlike substance. It is also called adipocere.

Other times, the body seems huge because it is bloated and there is nowhere for the gas to escape. This causes body parts to enlarge, sometimes giving a false impression of the size of the victim. It also causes the body to float to the surface.

Once the body reaches the morgue and the autopsy begins, the examiner needs to check the airway and lungs for water. In instances where the victim was killed before entering the water, there will be minimal amounts of water in the airway and lungs.

Whatever water is present in the body, whether a little or a lot, it is collected and sent to the lab for testing. There, scientists can obtain a control sample of the water and test it against the sample taken from the victim.

Introduction to Subject Matter

(to be read to students)

Microbes and diatoms play a major role in establishing a water source for bodies that have been dumped in an aquatic environment. Every such environment has its own set of microbes and diatoms. Investigators usually turn to a forensic biologist to identify these organisms and match them to a water source. Depending on the amount of water in the body, investigators can tell whether the person was alive before entering the water. The investigator can also make an educated guess from the condition of the body at the time of retrieval.

Vocabulary

Adipocere	A soft, unctuous, or waxy substance, of a light brown color, into which the fat and muscle tissue of dead bodies sometimes are converted by long immersion in water or by burial in a moist place; it is a result of fatty degeneration
Adipose	Fat found in tissue just below the skin and surrounding major organs, acting as an energy reserve and providing insulation and protection
Diatom	A microscopic unicellular marine or freshwater algae having siliceous cell walls
Lifeline	A rope that is secured to a diver when conducting a line search; the line is connected to someone on shore
Line search	A search that is conducted by arranging people side by side to search a suspected area for clues or a body
Microbe	A microscopic organism, especially a pathogenic species
Pulmonary edema	A characteristic of drowning that creates a white froth coming out of the mouth and nose
Saponification	The breaking down of oils into very fine droplets called colloids; hydrolyzing a fat with alkali to form a soap and glycerol

Lesson Objectives (with Standards Guide Words)

- Students will learn what microbes and diatoms are and illustrate examples. (Guide words: definition, comparison, contrast, writing, illustration)
- Students will learn about certain types of microbes and diatoms and illustrate examples. (Same guide words as preceding objective)
- Students will be able to identify microbes and diatoms under a microscope and illustrate examples. (Same guide words, plus: identification)
- Students will learn what saponification is and illustrate examples. (Guide words: definition, comparison, contrast, writing, illustration)

Lesson and Learning Activity

Allotted time: fifty minutes

Drowning in Thin Air

This past Monday morning at 6:00 A.M., the body of a young man was found lying in a field. The body was recovered by the medical examiner team and taken to the hospital for an autopsy. Upon incision, the doctor noticed a large amount of a watery substance in the lungs. The doctor extracted the water from the lungs and preserved it for further testing at the state crime lab. The doctor declared that the victim died from drowning (the official cause of death is called pulmonary edema). He also approximated his death to about twelve hours before he was found. This would mean that he was killed on Sunday evening around 6:00. How could someone drown on dry land?

After reading the autopsy results, investigators began trying to retrace the steps that led to the homicide. They knew that the victim was drowned, and there were several lakes and ponds within a ten-mile radius. They would have to sample all of the water sources in the area for crime lab comparison. Four water sources were sampled: Johnson Dam, Smith's Pond, Filbert's Pond, and Juniata's Pond.

Smith's Pond stuck out in their mind because they found a gray sweater on the side of the bank. The sweater belonged to the victim. Investigators later found out that the victim lived by Smith's Pond. At the present time, they do not have any suspects; so, for the time being, investigators want to find out in which pond he was drowned.

You need to supply:

> Four test tubes, each with a 10 ml sample of the pond waters taken; label each one for location
>
> One test tube filled with 5 ml of water from the victim's lungs (this sample should match with Filbert's Pond)
>
> Slides
>
> Cover slips
>
> Droppers
>
> Microscope
>
> Handout or overhead of diatoms and microbes

Have students work in groups to investigate the samples. Designate one student from each group for the samples. Another should be in charge of the microscope, and a third should be in charge of documenting the findings. They should be drawing pictures of the diatoms they see under the microscope.

After students have looked at all of the samples, there should be one sample with more microbes and diatoms in common with the suspect sample than the other ones. That will be your mystery water source!

	Drawing and Description
Sample A	
Sample B	
Sample C	
Sample D	

110   *Partners in Crime*

CRIME SCENE DO NOT CROSS CRIME SCENE DO NOT CROSS CRIME SCENE DO NOT CROSS CRIME SCENE DO NOT CROSS CRIME SCENE DO NOT CROSS CRIME SCENE DO NOT CROSS CRIME SCENE

Springboard to Writing

Allotted time: fifty minutes; three days for polished final paper

> On Saturday afternoon, two boys fishing in Pepper's Pond were not catching much. One of the boys decided to take a leisurely swim because the sun was particularly hot that day. As he was swimming, his buddy's line got snagged on the bottom. Not wanting to lose his favorite lure, he asked his friend to dive down and see if he could get his snag out. The boy agreed, took a deep breath, and plunged to the bottom. He came back up screaming that his lure was stuck on a body. He quickly swam to shore, where they ran home and told their story to their neighbor. She called 911 and soon police were on the scene.
>
> As the body was pulled to the surface, someone recognized the deceased as a twenty-year-old waiter who worked in the local restaurant. The body was properly secured and taken to the medical examiner. Detective Jamia Benson was new to the detectives unit and asked if she could sit in on the autopsy. The doctor approved and began his examination.

As the doctor, write a narrative discussion between you and the new detective, Benson. Explain to her what you are doing and why. Insert the questions in the list at appropriate places to assist in the discussion. These are questions the detective will be asking. Employ the information learned in the opening activity, and use quotation marks to create a dialogue between the two in narrative form. This activity should take approximately one class period to write. (*Aside for teacher:* You can make it a long-term assignment and have students type the paper and hand it in at a later date. Use the assessment to grade the paper.)

These questions from Detective Benson are not in order. It is up to you to use them in the correct order.

> How does someone drown?
>
> How do you know where the water came from?
>
> What is in the water that tells you where it came from?
>
> What are microbes and diatoms?
>
> Can you tell how long the body has been down there?
>
> How do you know the person did not die before entering the water?
>
> What is the point of placing the body in a body bag as soon as it comes out of the water?
>
> Who looks at the water samples?

CSI Notebook

Allotted time: ten minutes

The scenario presented here can be an unpleasant experience for some. Have students pretend they are Jamia Benson. Would they be able to sit through the autopsy? If they say yes, have them explain what aspects they would like in watching the autopsy. If students say no, why would they never want to attend an autopsy again?

Assessment

- **Mastery (A).** Student uses all questions provided and adds more. Student uses the formatting of quotations correctly (punctuation, spacing, and so on; see the sample given here).
- **Proficient (B).** Student uses all questions provided and does not add more. Student uses quotations correctly with punctuation.
- **Satisfactory (C).** Student uses half of the questions provided. Student has quotations but they are not punctuated correctly.
- **Unsatisfactory (D).** Student uses fewer than three of the questions provided. Student does not punctuate quotations at all.
- **Insufficient (F).** Student makes up own questions that are not related to the topic. Student does not have any quotations.

Here is a sample dialogue the medical examiner had with Detective Benson, written with properly formatted quotations.

When Detective Benson came into the morgue, she had a very curious look on her face. She said, "This is my first autopsy, Doc. Don't try to gross me out, because it won't work."

I replied, "OK, I won't."

"Good," she said. "Now, how do you know how long the body is down there and if the person really drowned?"

I told her about examining the condition of the body and that, taking into consideration the water temperature, I could estimate the time the body was down there by looking at the stage of decomposition.

"What happens when it sits down there for a while?" she blurted out.

"Well, first the body sinks to the bottom because all of the air is expired from the body. As the body decomposes, gases build up, and eventually it rises to the surface. If there has been any kind of cut, or blunt or sharp force trauma to the body, the gas might escape and the body could stay down there."

She looked at me with a satisfying nod.

"And," I said, "I can tell whether or not the person drowned, if there is any evidence of substantial water in the lungs and the presence of froth coming out of the nose and mouth, which is called pulmonary edema."

"Oh," she said as she bit her left index fingernail. "Well, what do you need to look for in your water examination?"

I explained to her about microbes and diatoms and how they can be matched to a certain water source. She looked at me with surprise. "I didn't know there were that many kinds of microorganisms in the world," she said.

"Oh yes, there are many of them and they all serve a different purpose," I said with a triumphant finger waving in the air.

"Yes, well, that's great and everything, but I don't need to know all of that right now," she said sarcastically.

"Detective, you did place this body directly in a body bag once brought ashore, right?"

112   *Partners in Crime*

CRIME SCENE DO NOT CROSS CRIME SCENE DO NOT CROSS CRIME SCENE DO NOT CROSS CRIME SCENE DO NOT CROSS CRIME SCENE DO NOT CROSS CRIME SCENE DO NOT CROSS CRIME SCENE

"Yes, I've heard all about how evidence is lost when bodies are thrown in the water. That's how some perps try to wash away evidence. Too bad for them the microbes and diatoms stick around after the show is over."

I chuckled at her sense of humor and realized that there was no way I would be able to shake this girl on her first autopsy, so we began.

Lesson Accommodations and Modifications

If students are not familiar with using quotations properly, have them draw a vertical line on their paper. One side will be what the examiner says and the other side will be what the detective says. This can be used as a graphic organizer. Then have them try to punctuate their paper without turning it into a paragraph. This way they can practice using quotation marks and correct punctuation. This works well for ESL students too.

For Further Study

If students are interested in taking this a step further, they can conduct their own experiments at home, grow their own microbes and diatoms, and bring them in to share with the class. You can assign extra credit or even use them for one of the case scenarios.

A student interested in becoming a forensic biologist will need a bachelor's degree in biology and special training in the lab for forensic aspects.

References

Bass, William. *Death's Acre: Inside the Legendary Forensic Lab/The Body Farm/Where the Dead Do Tell Tales*. New York: Putnam, 2003.

Budowle, Bruce. *DNA Typing Protocols: Molecular Biology and Forensic Analysis*. Natick, Mass.: Eaton, 2000.

Camenson, Blythe, and Huft, Anita. *Opportunities in Forensic Science Careers*. New York: McGraw Hill, 2001.

Dixon, Bernard. *Power Unseen*. New York: Oxford University Press, 1998.

Postgate, John. *Microbes and Man* (4th ed.). Cambridge, UK: Cambridge University Press, 2000.

Roach, Mary. *Stiff: The Curious Lives of Human Cadavers*. New York: Norton, 2003.

Spitz, Werner. *Spitz and Fisher Medico-Legal Investigation of Death* (3rd ed.). Springfield, Ill.: Charles C. Thomas, 1993.

Wolber, Charles. *Forensic Biology for the Law Enforcement Officer*. Springfield, Ill.: Charles C. Thomas, 1974.

Chapter Nine

Hair and Fiber Analysis

Overview for Teachers

Hair and fibers have played a major role in linking criminals to their crime. Edmund Locard was the first to establish the theory that "every contact leaves a trace." He set up a forensic lab in Lyons, France, in 1910. He was always fascinated by what he calls "the problem of dust." The word *dust* later came to represent what we now consider physical evidence left at a crime scene and the evidence that the perpetrator takes with him or her from the crime scene. Fibers from a trunk can rub off on a victim. Hairs found on a corpse can link a criminal to the crime. This has proved to be a valuable tool in catching criminals.

Hair

Hair identification is not absolute, but it is unlikely that two people have the same microscopic characteristics in their hair. If the root of the hair is intact, it can be subjected to DNA testing. Scientists can conclude that samples exhibit the same characteristics, which gives a stronger case for circumstantial evidence against a suspect. Matching the hair accurately depends on the type of hair analyzed. Hairs from the head are considered to be the best sample to use; they are usually the longest hair on the body. It can appear uncut, or if it has been altered it displays evidence in the slanted or flat end where the hair was cut. If there has been a struggle, the victim's or perpetrator's hair might appear kinked or crinkled.

Hair from the head can also be used to determine the race of a person. There are basic differences in characteristics that forensic scientists are aware of. Caucasian hairs range from round to oval in cross section; the pigment granules within the hair are usually fine to medium-sized. Asian hairs, by contrast, are in terms of outward appearance straight, coarse, and circular in cross section; the diameter is wider than for hairs of other racial groups. African American hairs are curly or kinked; they have a flattened appearance in cross section.

Dyes can also be noticed through microscopic evaluation. Head hair grows about one to two millimeters per week; under a microscope, the root of the hair shows the true color of the hair in the cortex.

Although hair from the head is best for comparison, there are other types of hair on the human body that have distinguishing characteristics. They can be placed in five other groups. Most of these characteristics can be seen in cross section, obtained by embedding the hair in wax and then slicing it in thin pieces to be viewed on a slide.

- **Eyelash or eyebrow hair.** Viewed under the microscope on a slide, the ends are usually tapered because they are not regularly cut. The cross section is usually circular in shape.
- **Body hair.** This is usually curly when laid out on a slide. The cross section appears to have a triangular or oval shape.
- **Underarm hair.** Cross-section has an oval appearance.
- **Facial hair.** This is usually curlier than head hear. The cross section often has a triangular shape.
- **Pubic hair.** This is springy or curly when laid out on a slide. The cross section has an oval or triangular appearance.

Another positive attribute about hair for our purposes is its resistance to chemical decomposition. It can retain structural features for a long time. Exhumed bodies still have the hair intact after many years of being buried in the ground. Among the structural features are the cuticle, which is the scaly exterior portion that distinguishes human from animal hair; the cortex, which gives the hair pigment; and the center of the hair, named the medulla (it can be classified as continuous, fragmented, or totally absent).

Fibers

Fibers are also important at a crime scene. A fiber is the smallest unit of a textile material that is longer than its diameter. Fibers can be natural or man-made. A fiber can be spun together with other fibers to create a yarn, which is then woven or knitted to form a fabric.

The type and length of fiber affect the "transfer" of a fiber at a crime scene. A fiber can be transferred in two ways. Primary transfer is when a fiber moves directly from a fabric onto a person's clothing. The second transference is secondary transfer, when a person picks up a fiber that has already been left somewhere.

Some common natural fibers are cotton, wool, and flax. They can be dyed for color change. Fine wool fibers are not too coarse and are used for clothing; the coarser wool fibers are used in carpet.

More than half of known fibers are man-made. Polyester and nylon fibers are the most common, though rayons, acrylics, and acetates are seen too. Specificity of man-made fibers can be seen in cross sections. Some are common while others are unique to one kind of manufacture.

Hair and fiber evidence is not a clincher for an attorney, but it presents more circumstantial evidence that the suspect was at the crime scene.

Hair and Fiber Analysis   **115**

CRIME SCENE DO NOT CROSS CRIME SCENE DO NOT CROSS CRIME SCENE DO NOT CROSS CRIME SCENE DO NOT CROSS CRIME SCENE DO NOT CROSS CRIME SCENE DO NOT CROSS CRIME SCENE DO NOT CROSS CRIME SCENE

Introduction to Subject Matter

(to be read to students)

Hair and fibers are used to help identify suspects or victims at the scene of the crime. They constitute excellent evidence. The "match" of a hair is not 100 percent, so an expert would testify in court that it has characteristics very similar to the crime scene sample shown. Fibers, on the other hand, can be analyzed for more exact information as far as dye and composition go. Knowledge of fibers is being used more and more in courts today.

Vocabulary

Acetate	A product made of ester cellulose ethanoate; it has a soft, crisp feel and silky appearance
Acrylic	A synthetic textile fiber produced from acrylonitrile
Cortex	Located at the bottom of the hair; imparts pigmentation
Cotton	A tropical or subtropical bush producing soft, white, downy fibers and oil-rich seeds; genus *Gossypium*
Cross section	A plane surface formed by cutting through an object at a right angle to an axis, especially the longest axis
Evidence transfer principle	Any two objects that come into contact leave a trace of each other
Exhumation	The process of disinterring a grave so further tests can be run on the body or it can be autopsied again
Flax	A plant with blue flowers that is widely cultivated for its seeds, which produce linseed oil, and its stems, from which the fiber to make linen is obtained; Latin name *Linum usitatissimum*
Medulla	The material that is located throughout the center of the hair
Nylon	A tough, synthetic material widely used in different forms in manufactured articles such as food containers, brush bristles, and clothing
Polyester	A strong, hard-wearing synthetic fabric with low moisture absorbency, made from a group of condensation polymers used to form synthetic fibers
Rayon	A fiber composed of regenerated cellulose, derived from wood pulp, cotton, linters, or other vegetable matter
Wool yarn	Spun from the short, curly hair of sheep or other mammals; used in knitting or weaving

116   *Partners in Crime*

CRIME SCENE DO NOT CROSS CRIME SCENE DO NOT CROSS CRIME SCENE DO NOT CROSS CRIME SCENE DO NOT CROSS CRIME SCENE DO NOT CROSS CRIME SCENE DO NOT CROSS CRIME SCENE

Lesson Objectives (with Standards Guide Words)

- Students will explore the evidence transfer principle and illustrate examples. (Guide words: evidence definition, comparison, contrast, writing, illustration)

- Students will differentiate a human hair from an animal hair and illustrate examples. (Same guide words as preceding objective)

- Students will be able to identify fibers on the basis of microscopic evaluation and illustrate examples. (Same guide words)

- Students will be able to identify the cortex of a hair and illustrate examples. (Same guide words)

- Students will be able to determine the difference between hairs from two bodies and illustrate examples. (Same guide words)

- Students will be able to identify dyed hair under a microscope and illustrate examples. (Same guide words)

- Students will learn to identify fibers on the basis of microscopic comparison and illustrate examples. (Same guide words)

Lesson and Learning Activity

Allotted time: preparation, one hour; activity, fifty minutes

Who Stole the Cure?

On Sunday morning, April 25, 2004, Advantis Laboratories reported two missing vials of a special vaccine that was designed to fight cancer. Advantis was one of the world's leading labs in creating this vaccine. It was extremely expensive and Advantis was the only company with a patent for it. Police were called in to investigate.

The crime scene occurred in Lab A, where the completed vials were stored. After the crime scene was secured, investigators began looking for evidence to collect and label. They started at the area where the vials were taken. On the floor in front of the counter where the empty vial holders were, a shoe print was found. Next to the footprint was a broken vial with white powder. Investigators decided the thief stepped in the powder accidentally after dropping the vial. Samples of the powder were collected and labeled for lab testing.

Another piece of evidence was found on the refrigerator handle. It had previously been broken, creating a sharp edge on the bottom side of the handle. There, investigators found what looked like fuzzy blue fibers. The refrigerator was used to store new batches of vaccine until they were ready for shipment. However, that particular day was not a day when new batches were placed in the refrigerator, so it was empty. Investigators carefully removed the fibers from the sharp edge and placed them in an evidence bag.

In the trash can by the door, investigators found a head cover, which was used by lab technicians to keep their hair from contaminating samples. Investigators discovered three strands of brown hair about four inches in length inside the head cover. These were also bagged and labeled.

For the final part of the investigation, investigators began dusting for prints. (You'll recall that this is the last part of collecting evidence because the black powder is messy and can contaminate evidence.) After persistently dusting countertops and other surfaces, investigators revealed a partial fingerprint on the door to the lab. They determined that the thief took off his or her gloves before leaving. No gloves were found in the lab.

Investigators began interviewing employees and checking entry logs. Because it was the night shift, few people were in the building. They narrowed their investigation down to four suspects.

Suspect one: John Woodruff
The night janitor of the building, he has been working there for five months. He recently transferred from another company that specializes in pharmaceuticals. After interviewing him, investigators found out that he had left his job for an increase in salary. Coworkers described him as a quiet kind of guy; he did not talk much while working. His Walkman was always blaring away while he cleaned. John is six feet tall, with brown hair. His blue uniform was standard, which all janitors are required to wear for their shift.

Suspect two: Jane Bocelli
Jane is a newly hired chemist who just graduated from the University of Pennsylvania. She is excited to be at a new job where she can work in the lab and solve the problems of the world. Recently, she has been working double shifts to help increase production of the new cancer vaccine. Coworkers described her as very friendly and enthusiastic. She is dedicated to her job and the world of medicine. She also wears heavy wool and fleece sweaters.

Suspect three: Jack Goodman
Jack was a long-time employee of the company; he had been working there for twenty years. He slowly worked his way up in the company but was recently passed over for a promotion to team leader for Lab A. He was highly disappointed and quite upset about it. Coworkers described him as a disgruntled individual. He did not talk much, and when he did it was usually to complain about something. Jack had worked on the team that developed the vaccine. He was rather annoyed that he did not get the job because of the time he had spent on the project. He is almost bald, but he does have short brown hair that is starting to turn gray.

118

Partners in Crime

CRIME SCENE DO NOT CROSS CRIME SCENE DO NOT CROSS CRIME SCENE DO NOT CROSS CRIME SCENE DO NOT CROSS CRIME SCENE DO NOT CROSS CRIME SCENE DO NOT CROSS CRIME SCENE

Suspect four: Corinne Svedorski

Corinne is a young woman who has been working with the company for three years. She holds a doctorate in chemistry, but she couldn't find the job she wanted. She took this job in hopes of moving up in the company. Corinne was overqualified for the job, but she figured she would pay her dues until she could get something better. Coworkers described her as a hard worker, usually putting in hours until late at night. Also, she was reprimanded several times recently for not wearing her head cover; her long brown hair contaminated a few vials of the vaccine.

All of these people are considered suspects in the case. Until lab results come back, they are instructed to not leave town. Who would steal this vaccine that could save the world? It is up to you, the detective to solve the case of the missing vials. Good luck!

Now, as teacher, you need to acquire four samples of hair and fiber.

Label the hair samples A, B, C, and D; this should be done before class. A sample must also be created. Corinne Svedorski is the guilty party in this scenario, so make sure her samples match up. Students should use copies of the table given on page 119 to document their findings.

Provide four fiber samples and label them A, B, C, and D. This should also be done before class. Have students use the table on page 120 to document their findings. Students will be able to match Corinne with the hair and fiber samples. Before you let the answer out, tell them that after Corinne was confronted with the evidence, she confessed in hopes of a lesser sentence.

Hair Samples	Drawings
Sample 1	
Sample 2	
Sample 3	
Sample 4	

Fiber Samples	Drawings
Sample 1	
Sample 2	
Sample 3	
Sample 4	

Springboard to Writing

Allotted time: fifty minutes

Tell the students that when court time comes around, they will be representing the defense. They want to try to get Corinne Svedorski off on anything possible; it's their job. Give students copies of the following statements taken at the police station. Have students proofread the depositions for mistakes in subject-verb agreement and tense changes. Students want to find mistakes in the writing and possibly expose the writer as a liar. You can turn this into a short quiz and grade students on the number of mistakes they find, and if they can correct them. This covers the areas of grammatical conventions and punctuation. Use the assessment for grading.

Along with this activity, use a tape recorder and have four people recite the confessions that are written out here. Students can then listen to the recordings while reading along with their handouts. Students will find that people do not always pronounce words the way they are spelled. Sometimes they tend to blend words or sounds together that sound different when written. For example, if you write, "Did you eat?" Everyone understands the context of the sentence. If spoken, it may sound more like "jeet." That is the same context, but the words are combined. Have students think of other examples of this happening, and write them on the board.

Statement Form

Name: John Woodruff   DOB/age: 12/12/75   29 yrs.   Case no.: 81812

Address: 543 Winter Ave, Jackson, NY 89393

Telephone: 555–1325   Date: April 26, 2004

Place of interview: Local police station

Beginning time: 12:13 p.m.   Ending time: 12:32 p.m.

Officer: _____

Signature: _____

Statement: I been hear for a couple months now. I worked in another place for a while, but then they asked if I wanted to work at Advantis. I said sure so I start working the next day. I like nighttime shifts so noone bother me. I like my walkman loud to. It blasts away all night and nonoe bother me. I was busy cleaning the night the vaccine got stolen. I don't pay attention to the workers in the building. They don't bother me and I doesn't bother them. Anyways like I says I was mopping and blasting my walkman. I was wearing my blue uniform with all cleaning people wear at work. I didn't here or sea anything.

Signature: *John Woodruff*   Date: 4/26/04   Time: 12:32 p.m.

Statement Form

Name: Jane Bocelli   DOB/age: 3/5/76   28 yrs.   Case no.: 81812

Address: 74 Kitty Way, Honedell, NY 83542

Telephone: 555–9037   Date: April 26, 2004

Place of interview: Local police station

Beginning time: 1:00 p.m.   Ending time: 1:15 p.m.

Officer: _____

Signature: _____

Statement: I was in the room with the vaccine for most of the evening. I did go on break at 3:30. I stopped in the cafeteria to have a chicken sandwich that I brought for dinner. After my sandwich, I returned to the lab and it was in the same condition I left it; perfect. I must admit that I fell asleep for about half an hour because I have been working double shifts lately. I have just begun to work here and I love what I do. I am so excited to finally be working with a team of experts who are dead-set on making a difference in the world. Working hard as I usually do, I did not see anyone enter or exit the room. When my shift was done, all was well and I left. I do not know if anyone else was planning on going into the room.

Signature: *Jane Bocelli*   Date: 4/26/04   Time: 1:15 p.m.

Statement Form

Name: Jack Goodman   DOB/age: 7/17/53   51 yrs.   Case no.: 81812

Address: 570 Palace Drive, Chalfint, NY 84396

Telephone: 555–8766   Date: April 26, 2004

Place of interview: Local police station

Beginning time: 1:53 p.m.   Ending time: 2:30 p.m.

Officer: _____

Signature: _____

Statement: I don't now why I'm hear. I have been hear fro twenty years now. They think they can hire these young people to do my job. I have the most experience out of everyone in the lab and I should be the one running the show and I was at home the night the vaccine was stolen. I know nothing about it. I was by myself. So nobody can vouch for me. I never lie about anything. Why would I steel a vaccine that I helped make. There is no way I would do something like that. I think you should look at the new girl Jane. I see her talking to that janitor guy the jerk who never says boo too anyone. You should check his background and find out why he really left that job. That's all I got to say.

Signature: *Jack Goodman*   Date: 4/26/04   Time: 2:30 p.m.

Statement Form

Name: Corinne Svedorski   DOB/age: 9/22/77   27 yrs.   Case no.: 81812

Address: 7754 Clifton Rd., Chalfint, NY 84396

Telephone: 555-9933   Date: April 26, 2004

Place of interview: Local police station

Beginning time: 3:17 p.m.   Ending time: 3:38 p.m.

Officer: _____

Signature: _____

Statement: I was working late the night the vaccine was absconded from the laboratory. Completing and documenting my reports is tedious work, but it is of paramount importance they are finished. I entered the laboratory at 3:35 to check the status of some vial I had placed in the refrigeration unit earlier on in the evening. I took notice that everything appeared normal. At 3:40, I returned to my office. I distinctly remember the time because I had to write a time on the log list when I left the lab. All personnel are required to sign the log list. Several of the irresponsible employees have not furnished the log with a signature lately; more specifically, Jane Bocelli. I have reprimanded her time and time again for not completing her mandatory duties as a lab assistant. I left the building at 4:35 a.m. and went home.

Signature: *Corinne Svedorski*   Date: 4/26/04   Time: 3:38 p.m.

126   *Partners in Crime*

CRIME SCENE DO NOT CROSS CRIME SCENE DO NOT CROSS CRIME SCENE DO NOT CROSS CRIME SCENE DO NOT CROSS CRIME SCENE DO NOT CROSS CRIME SCENE DO NOT CROSS CRIME SCENE

CSI Notebook

Allotted time: fifteen minutes

Have students write about hair and fibers. They should list the various kinds of hair and how they can be categorized. They should also be able to name the two kinds of fibers, how they are produced, and how they are classified by use of a microscope. This activity can be written as bullet points instead of full sentences.

Assessment

- **Mastery (A).** Student finds and corrects all mistakes of fact.
- **Proficient (B).** Student finds and corrects all but four mistakes.
- **Satisfactory (C).** Student finds and corrects all but eight mistakes.
- **Unsatisfactory (D).** Student finds and corrects all but ten mistakes.
- **Insufficient (F).** Student does not find any mistakes.

Lesson Accommodations and Modifications

Students who do not have the grammatical background will find this assignment difficult.

Instead, use the tape and see if they can transcribe at least five sentences from one of the spoken statements. Then have them underline words that sound different from how they are spelled. Students can make a T-chart to document differences. The ESL teacher should come to the class to work with those students.

For Further Study

Students who take an interest in this chapter should consider looking at sample fibers brought from home to see if they can identify them. If a student has a microscope at home, the identifications can be made there. If not, take the first five minutes of class and allow students to use a microscope in the classroom. Also have them bring several samples so other students can look too.

If a person wants to be a hair and fiber expert, he or she must first obtain a bachelor's degree in the field of criminology or forensic science. Then on-the-job training for approximately two years under the supervision of an expert is sufficient.

Cumulative Mystery

Allotted time: preparation, one hour; activity, two days

Day One

You need to prepare the three sample slides of hair taken from the house. Then prepare three more slides and label them A, B, and C (for Biff, Magnus, and Cliff, respectively).

Have students use the tables given here for comparisons. Biff's and Magnus's hair should match two of the samples; Cliff's hair does not match any.

Hair Samples from Crime Scene	Drawings
Sample 1	
Sample 2	
Sample 3	

Hair Samples	Drawings
Sample 1	
Sample 2	
Sample 3	

Hair and Fiber Analysis

129

CRIME SCENE DO NOT CROSS CRIME SCENE DO NOT CROSS CRIME SCENE DO NOT CROSS CRIME SCENE DO NOT CROSS CRIME SCENE DO NOT CROSS CRIME SCENE DO NOT CROSS CRIME SCENE

Crime Scene Samples

Detectives also took samples of carpet from each room. There were a total of three kinds of carpet fibers in Jackie's house, in beige, red, and green. The beige belonged in the living room and dining room; the red carpet was in the bedroom, and the green was from a floor mat in the bathroom.

Police discovered some brown hairs around the sink, approximately five inches in length. They were bagged and sent to the lab. Also, Jackie's hairbrush was bagged and sent to the lab as a control sample.

At the lab, three different hair samples were examined, one of which belonged to Jackie. The other two were still unidentified as the scientist waited until the next day. Police called the three suspects to the station. Biff and Magnus willingly and gladly agreed to give hair samples for comparison. Biff even stated that some of the hairs on Jackie's brush would match his since he used her brush several times while at her house. Cliff, on the other hand, was a little reluctant to give any sample until the detective mentioned a court order. He gave in and provided the hair sample.

You should do the lab now.

Day Two

Prepare three slides taken from the house—red, green, and beige—and label them respectively 1, 2, and 3. Then prepare two sample slides of the red and green fibers found in Biff's car and label them A and B. Students will be able to make a match to the fibers taken from the house.

Samples from Biff's Car

Since Cliff's hair did not match, the detectives decided to put him on the back burner for now to focus instead on Biff and Magnus. They obtained search warrants.

At Biff's house, detectives did not find anything out of the ordinary. After an exhaustive search, they turned to his car. The first thing they did was photograph his tire treads to compare to the sample cast made at the crime scene. On one of his floor mats, they found some traces of red and green fibers. These were collected and sent to the lab.

Magnus's house did not turn up any evidence. His tires were also photographed and sent to the lab for comparison. Magnus mentioned that his tracks were definitely at the house because he worked there. Police told him to stay put for a while and not to make any long-term plans.

At the lab, scientists conducted a fiber analysis on the two fibers found in Biff's car. Have the students use the tables on pages 130 and 131.

All the evidence is pointing to Biff. Although the evidence is circumstantial, detectives are keeping a very close eye on him.

Fiber Samples from Crime Scene	Drawings
Sample 1	
Sample 2	
Sample 3	

Samples Taken from Biff's Car	Drawings
Red Fiber	
Green Fiber	

132   *Partners in Crime*

CRIME SCENE DO NOT CROSS CRIME SCENE DO NOT CROSS CRIME SCENE DO NOT CROSS CRIME SCENE DO NOT CROSS CRIME SCENE DO NOT CROSS CRIME SCENE DO NOT CROSS CRIME SCENE

References

American Chemical Society. *Forensic Science: A Project of the Education Division of the American Chemical Society.* New York: Freeman, 2001.

Camenson, Blythe, and Huft, Anita. *Opportunities in Forensic Science Careers.* New York: McGraw-Hill, 2001.

Conklin, Barbara G., Gardner, Robert, and Shortelle, Dennis. *Encyclopedia of Forensic Science.* Phoenix: Oryx, 2002.

Evans, Colin. *The Casebook of Forensic Detection: How Science Solved 100 of the World's Most Baffling Crimes.* Hoboken, N.J.: Wiley, 1998.

Graver, Anne. *Bodies of Evidence: Reconstructing History Through Skeletal Analysis.* Hoboken, N.J.: Wiley, 1995.

Lee, Henry, and O'Neill, Thomas. *Cracking Cases: The Science of Solving Crimes.* New York: Prometheus, 2002.

Maples, William. *Dead Men Do Tell Tales.* New York: Broadway Books, 1994.

Miller, Hugh. *What the Corpse Revealed: Murder and the Science of Forensic Detection.* New York: St. Martin's Press, 1999.

Nickell, John. *Crime Science: Methods of Forensic Detection.* Lexington: University Press of Kentucky, 1999.

Owen, David. *Hidden Evidence.* Richmond Hill, Ontario: Firefly Books, 2000.

Chapter Ten

Handwriting Analysis

Overview for Teachers

Handwriting analysis has been used for hundreds of years. Forgers have been in the business for a long time and have made fortunes doing it. Some students display this ability when a test or document is returned with a signature that is fake. Some get caught and others get away with it.

Introduction to Subject Matter

(to be read to students)

Have you ever tried to copy a signature or turn in a paper with a forged signature? That is where forgers begin their career. If they can pull it off in school, why not make a career out of it? There are many instances of forgery throughout history. Sometimes document examiners spot mistakes and catch criminals, while other times the cheaters are still out there, forging everything from checks to discipline referrals that go home. The activities in this chapter bring better understanding of how to spot a forgery.

Vocabulary

Document analysis	The process of determining whether or not a document is forged
Leaking	The process of ink leaking out, creating a mark, usually a round dot, when a person stops or hesitates while writing
Slope	To be at, or have, an angle that deviates from horizontal
Smearing	A smudge on the paper left as a person drags the palm in the ink that has not dried

Lesson Objectives (with Standards Guide Words)

- Students will learn the term *document analysis*. (Guide words: document analysis, writing process, definition, application)

134   *Partners in Crime*

CRIME SCENE DO NOT CROSS CRIME SCENE DO NOT CROSS CRIME SCENE DO NOT CROSS CRIME SCENE DO NOT CROSS CRIME SCENE DO NOT CROSS CRIME SCENE DO NOT CROSS CRIME SCENE

- Students will recognize patterns in handwriting. (Same guide words as preceding objective, plus: patterns, word formations)
- Students will identify various structural changes in handwriting. (Guide words: document analysis, writing process, definition, application)
- Students will learn to match a sample of writing to the original author. (Same guide words as preceding objective, plus: structure, letter formations)
- Students will identify the categories used to identify handwriting. (Guide words: document analysis, writing process, definition, application)

Lessons and Learning Activities

Allotted time: activity one, fifty minutes; activity two, thirty-five minutes

These activities can be done in English class. Studying a person's handwriting is called graphology. People have writing styles as individual as their fingerprints. Even if someone is injured and the writing hand sustains an injury, he or she will learn to write with the other hand and develop the same characteristics of writing. There are also specialists who claim that one's personality is revealed through his or her writing. There is published literature to that effect, but it is not accepted in the courtroom.

Activity One: Analysis of Handwriting

Have students complete a short writing piece (in script) made up of the four sentences given here. Do not tell them that they will be looking at handwriting, or some students will not give you the best examples of their handwriting. Use these sentences:

1. The way you fidget with that gadget makes me nervous.
2. I also want to know what time the train leaves the station.
3. The righteous will retain their innocence.
4. For the fourth time, I don't know where the film was filmed.

After they have finished, each student should switch papers with a partner. What are some immediate differences that can be noticed? Have students generate one main list on the board. Here are some areas that you can use for identifying characteristics in writing.

When students learn to write, they start with drawing or copying letters that you write on the board. There are usually three lines on the tracing paper: top, middle, and bottom. These three areas can be used for analyzing handwriting.

Look at the letter *a*. In most cases, students have been taught to make a complete circle around, closing off the top, and finishing with the upstroke to the middle of the line. When students begin writing letters instead of copying them, they begin to

Handwriting Analysis   **135**

CRIME SCENE DO NOT CROSS CRIME SCENE DO NOT CROSS CRIME SCENE DO NOT CROSS CRIME SCENE DO NOT CROSS CRIME SCENE DO NOT CROSS CRIME SCENE DO NOT CROSS CRIME SCENE

develop their own writing style. In the case of the *a,* is the top closed? Is there a space where the writer retraces over the starting point? Does the upstroke come to the middle? If used in a word, how is the *a* connected to the next letter? Is it a smooth curve, or more pointed? These are just a few variations of looking at single letter developments and their variations in written form.

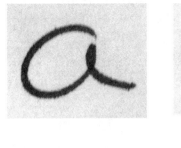

Another area to look at is the slope of the writing. Students can use a transparent protractor to measure the angle of letters. In this case, tall letters (*t, f, h, l*) should be used. Have students look at the slope of the four examples of the letter *t* and chart them using the three designated areas top, middle, and bottom.

The next area for study is the formation of letters. Have students focus on one letter in the writing. Using the guidelines for the letter *a,* do the same thing; look at the amount of straight lines, curves, and angles used.

Look at the examples (on page 136) of full word formation. What are the similarities and differences among these samples of *lake* and *day?* (Matches: 1 and 7; 2 and 8; 3 and 9; 4 and 10; 5 and 11; no match for 6) Can you have students match up instances of *lake* and *day* with the first two letters *a* presented in this chapter?

Another area that can be considered is the use of writing instrument. Some pens tend to "leak" when the writer stops or starts a word. This is sometimes represented by a small dot where the pen is placed on the paper and leaks a little. Also, some writers who do not lift the pen all the way off the paper while writing leave ink streaks where the pen has touched the paper in between words.

Smearing happens more with left-handed writers than right-handed ones because as the edge of the palm touches the paper, it may smear the words that have just been written. A right-handed person can do it too, though, by smearing the previous lines while dragging the edge of the palm or the little finger.

136   *Partners in Crime*

CRIME SCENE DO NOT CROSS CRIME SCENE DO NOT CROSS CRIME SCENE DO NOT CROSS CRIME SCENE DO NOT CROSS CRIME SCENE DO NOT CROSS CRIME SCENE DO NOT CROSS CRIME SCENE

Activity Two

This activity deals with looking at writing and differences in individual patterns. The important point here is for students to pick up on variations that exist among samples. When students ask for specific directions (which they will), tell them to just follow the instructions they are given. There is no right or wrong.

Step one. Distribute a plain white sheet of composition paper to each student. Have the student rip the paper into four pieces. You should make note of the differences in how the paper has been torn. Some students go lengthwise, and others widthwise. Mention this to the class.

Step two. Have the students label the pieces with the numerals one through four. Note the difference in where the person writes the number on the paper. Some might also be circled, or be followed by a period, or preceded by the "#" sign, or even written in roman numerals. Mention differences to the class.

Step three. Have each student sign his or her name in script on pieces one and two. Then have them superimpose the pieces on top of one another and compare them (this works best if held up to the light). Are the signatures exactly the same? What differences are there?

Step four. Using sheet three, have students try to *copy* one of their own signatures from number one or two. When they are finished, have them superimpose the copy over the original. What differences are there? Are there any hesitation marks? This is common in forged signatures.

Step five. Using sheet four, have students try to *trace* number one or two. Again, have students note the differences in the two. Sheet four should look rickety and jagged, because of hesitation.

Step six. Have students rip up the four pieces and place them in little bags, one bag given to each student. After they have jumbled the pieces of paper, ask them to put their pieces back together like a puzzle.

A great follow-up activity is to secretly plant a ripped-up note on the floor or in a book underneath the desk before the class comes in. You should have a student write the letter (not the teacher) because students can recognize your writing rather easily. (You should have the student write something silly and unimportant, to avoid any conflict among students.) The letter should contain some words that students use as part of their everyday lingo. Sometime during the class period, "stumble" across the note, or have one of the students open a book to find the mess. Explain to them that it looks like a student note. Once they see some of their own jargon in there, they will be more eager to put the note together and read it.

Springboard to Writing

Allotted time: twenty-five minutes

The Case of the Bad Check

On Friday afternoon, May 7, 2004, George Johannsen, the bank president, cashed a check for a new customer. The check was written to one Ingrid McWhorter for $1,000.00. He processed the transaction and paid the money to Ingrid.

The following Tuesday rolled around and a long-time customer, Brian Hasslock, came storming into the bank demanding to see Johannsen. Hasslock claimed that he had noticed on an online bank statement that the bank had apparently cashed a check on his account for $1,000.00. Hasslock said he never issued such a check and demanded to know whom the check was written out to. Johannsen went into the back and retrieved the check. It was written out to Ingrid McWhorter, for the amount of $1,000.00. It was dated and signed by Brian Hasslock himself. Hasslock *snapped at Johannsen that Ingrid was one of his workers (he owned a company that grew worms for fishermen). As he looked closely at the check, he noticed a dirty fingerprint on it. Hasslock took the check and returned to his warehouse.*

Inside the musty building, he headed right for the area where Ingrid worked on her worm beds. He grabbed her by the arm and marched her to his office. He slammed the door and insisted on an answer as to why she would do something like that. She had been working there for twenty years, producing some of the juiciest worms he had ever seen. Ingrid immediately denied having written the check. As tears streamed down her face, Hasslock came to believe her. Then it clicked in his mind. There were three other women in the warehouse who had access to the checkbook: Katrina Tamasso, Nikole Hedderon, and Mary Cooper. He gathered all of them, brought them to his office, and called his close friend Detective Bill Kahil to come over to investigate.

Kahil asked each secretary to provide a writing sample. He asked them to write this sentence: "Old McDonald went camping and bass fishing at the Farian dock." He also instructed them to write in cursive. Each one did as told and handed it over to the detective. He also took fingerprints of each suspect in case he needed further evidence for testing.

*After all the women left the room, Hasslock questioned what that sentence had to do with anything. Kahil explained that he did not want them to write the exact words that were on the check. Instead, he chose words that have similar word replications (*McDonald *and* McWhorter, camping *and the* -ng *in* Ingrid, Farian *and* Brian, bass *and* Hasslock, *and* dock *and* lock *as in* Hasslock*).*

Kahil lined up the samples next to the check. Using a magnifying glass, he began to match up similarities and differences between the samples and the forged check. Who was it?

Make copies of the form and the blank check on page 140. Have several fellow teachers fill out a copy of the check and write the "Old MacDonald" sentence in the statement area. You fill out the top section of each statement form. Then make copies of one of the checks and a copy of all the completed statement forms. Have students find at least four points that match up from one statement form and the check. You can also rotate the checks for different results. (Mary Cooper will be the person forging the check.)

Informative Piece

Allotted time: two days

Using the same scenario, have students write a process piece on how Detective Kahil examines the handwriting. Students should think about the various ways to study and examine handwriting. Also ask them to think about transitions in a paper. Have them generate a list of words that can be used to show transition between sentences and paragraphs, and within a sentence. Discuss as well where a transition should be placed in a paragraph for the best flow. Use the assessment for grading.

Here is some input to model transition words for the class.

Comparing and Contrasting Ideas

also	another	similarly
although	but	too
and	however	yet

Showing Cause and Effect in Narration

as a result	for	so that
because	since	therefore

Showing Time in Narration

after	first, second, etc.	then
before	following	until
finally	next	when

Showing Place in Description

above	down	next
around	here	over
before	in	there
beside	into	under

Sample Essay

Brandon Hoelle, Period 2

Analyzing handwriting can be quite a difficult task. The examiner needs some things to look for and observe. One of these areas is to observe individual letters and how they are formed. Another area is to look at a string of words and see how they are connected. As in the case of the bad check, Detective Kahil must first see the evidence. Then he needs to decide which words or letters should be duplicated to use for comparison. Although a lengthy process, a positive match can be made.

Statement Form

Name: _____ DOB/age: _____ Case number: _____

Address: _____

_____

Telephone: _____ Date: _____

Place of interview: _____

Beginning time: _____ Ending time: _____

Officer: _____ Signature: _____

Statement: _____

_____

_____

_____

_____

_____

_____

_____

_____

_____

Signature: _____ Date: _____ Time: _____

Hasslock Worm Industries	**0095743**
432 Indian Terrace	
Sparta, NJ 00943	_____ , 20 ____ $\frac{12\text{-}345}{6789}$

Pay to the
order of _____ $ [.]

_____ Dollars

FIRST BANK OF SPARTA
        Sparta, NJ

Memo _____   _____

First Detective Kahil needs to look at the evidence, which is the check itself. It was made out to an Ingrid McWhorter and signed by a Brian Hasslock. It was written for the amount of $1,000.00 and dated May 7, 2004. The writing needs to be studied carefully first for similarities and differences in the signature of Brian Hasslock and the signature of Brian Hasslock on the bad check. Detective Kahil should make notes and photograph the two side by side.

Now the interesting part begins. He needs to round up the suspects and take a writing sample. A sentence needs to be designed to include some of the letters and strings of letters to be compared to the forged check. From the two names, Ingrid McWhorter and Brian Hasslock, the detective will have the suspects write the sentence, "Old McDonald went camping and bass fishing at the Farian dock." With these samples, Detective Kahil can now begin comparing the handwriting.

What needs to be done first is look at the "Mc" in McDonald and compare it with the McWhorter. How are the "M" and "c" formed? Using a magnifying glass, Detective Kahil should be able to see resemblances and differences between the two. He should take notes and pictures if possible for future reference. Next, Detective Kahil can compare the "ng" in camping and fishing with the "ng" in Ingrid. He should follow the same process as above. Then he should look at the word "bass" and compare it with "Hasslock." Next, he should look at the "ian" in Farian and the "ian" in Brian. Finally, he should look at the "ock" in dock and the "ock" in Hasslock. Once the tests are finished, he should be able to make a conclusive decision about who the forger is.

By following the above steps, Detective Kahil should be able to decide who the culprit is and make an arrest. He must also remember to follow the correct steps in completing the process. Looking at the evidence is important so the examiner can decide what kind of sentence to have the suspects write. Finally, he or she should know what parts of the letter or strings of letters to examine for a positive identification.

CSI Notebook

Allotted time: twenty minutes
Have five students come to the board and write the phrase "flight in a wagon." Have students write about the differences in the handwriting, citing examples from the lesson. Students can share notes and come to the board to demonstrate for the class where the similarities and differences are.

Assessment

• **Mastery (A).** Student has smooth and fluent transitions from one idea to another. Student provides logical order to identifying letter formations. Student gives examples with elaborate detail.

142   *Partners in Crime*

CRIME SCENE DO NOT CROSS CRIME SCENE DO NOT CROSS CRIME SCENE DO NOT CROSS CRIME SCENE DO NOT CROSS CRIME SCENE DO NOT CROSS CRIME SCENE DO NOT CROSS CRIME SCENE

- **Proficient (B).** Student has smooth transitions between paragraphs, but not within a paragraph itself. Student provides an adequate order to identifying letter formations. Student gives examples with sufficient detail.
- **Satisfactory (C).** Student has ideas, but transitions are not evident in every paragraph. Transitions are choppy from paragraph to paragraph. Student provides an order of identifying letter formations in a confusing manner. Student gives examples with limited detail.
- **Unsatisfactory (D).** Student does not have complete ideas and they do not appear in order. There are no apparent transitions between thoughts or paragraphs. Student gives no examples or detail.
- **Insufficient (F).** Student writes about the scenario or tells a story of another kind of forgery.

Lesson Accommodations and Modifications

Students who are not proficient in creating transitions may have difficulty with this writing piece. Start with the lists of transition words given earlier and ask students if they can find some of these words in the sample essay. Have them circle the words in the essay. Then have them write their sample piece and highlight areas that they think are appropriate for transition words. Ask them to choose from the list of transition words. This works well for ESL students too. The ESL teacher might want to write them in the margin of the student's paper for easier access.

For Further Study

If students are interested in learning more about handwriting analysis, they can find several books to read or do research on the Internet. They can also conduct their own experiments with family and friends. The information learned in the classroom can go a long way at home or while at a friend's house.

If a person is interested in becoming a forensic document examiner, he or she needs a bachelor's degree in any discipline for an entry-level position. Once in the lab, a person needs training in courses involving criminal justice, police science, or a criminalistics program. A two-year apprenticeship served under the watchful eye of a qualified examiner is usually the norm for training.

Cumulative Mystery

Allotted time: ten minutes

Before class, you should prepare three writing samples and a copy of the note. To make it more real, write the note on a piece of paper and then crumple it up and place it in an evidence bag. Do this for each group. Then photocopy the sentence written by each one of the suspects.

Handwriting Analysis **143**

CRIME SCENE DO NOT CROSS CRIME SCENE DO NOT CROSS CRIME SCENE DO NOT CROSS CRIME SCENE DO NOT CROSS CRIME SCENE DO NOT CROSS CRIME SCENE DO NOT CROSS CRIME SCENE

Tell the students to think back to Chapter Seven (on toxicology) as the mystery resumes.

The detectives found a crumpled note in the trash can at Jackie's house. It read, "I hate you and you will never get away with this. I am watching you, Jackie." Detectives also took writing samples from Biff, Magnus, and Cliff while they were at the police station. They had each suspect write this sentence: "If I ever have to find a way out of here, I will take you with me and bring my watch." Using the writing samples, try to match the writing to one of the three. (Aside for teacher: *It should match up with Cliff; use the statement form seen earlier in this chapter.)*

References

Armend, Karen. *Handwriting Analysis.* Franklin Lakes, N.J.: New Page Books, 1986.

Conklin, Barbara G., Gardner, Robert, and Shortelle, Dennis. *Encyclopedia of Forensic Science.* Phoenix: Oryx, 2002.

Ellen, David. *The Scientific Examination of Documents: Methods and Techniques* (2nd ed.). New York: Taylor and Francis, 1997.

Hilton, Ordway. *Scientific Examination of Questioned Documents* (rev. ed.). Lanham, Md.: Rowman and Littlefield, 1992.

Huber, Roy, and Headrick, Alfred. *Handwriting Identification: Facts and Fundamentals.* New York: CRC, 1999.

Levinson, Jay. *Questioned Documents: A Lawyer's Handbook.* Durham, N.C.: Academic Press, 2000.

McNichol, Andrea, and Nelson, Jeff. *Handwriting Analysis: Putting It to Work for You.* New York: McGraw-Hill, 1994.

Morris, Ron. *Forensic Handwriting Identification: Fundamental Concepts and Principles.* Durham, N.C.: Academic Press, 2000.

Nickell, John. *Crime Science: Methods of Forensic Detection.* Lexington: University Press of Kentucky, 1999.

Owen, David. *Hidden Evidence.* Richmond Hill, Ontario: Firefly Books, 2000.

Zonderman, John. *Beyond the Crime Lab.* Hoboken, N.J.: Wiley, 1999.

Chapter Eleven
Tool Mark Analysis

Overview for Teachers

Tool mark evidence enters the picture when there is a burglary, tire tracks, firearms, bullet casings, fingerprints, or a homicide involving blunt force trauma. *Tool marks* refers to anything that makes an impression on a surface. They will also show on the body as a result of blunt force trauma or any kind of assault. Remember that no two things are manufactured in exactly the same way, or wear exactly the same way, or break in exactly the same way. As examples, see the seven tool mark impressions of a tire iron and the five tool marks of a screwdriver on pages 146–148.

The most important method used in tool mark analysis is microscopy. The comparison microscope allows two items to be viewed simultaneously. Evidence projectiles, casings, and other items bearing tool marks are compared to known items in order to determine consistency or inconsistency, both in class characteristics and individual characteristics.

Tool marks can easily be made with Silly-Putty, or if your budget allows Mikrosil can be purchased from any crime scene company. Silly-Putty does not give as much clarity as Mikrosil.

Ask local detectives to come in to give a demonstration on casting tool marks. They can give students background information and casting material for use in the class.

Introduction to Subject Matter

(to be read to students)
When one object comes in contact with another, a transfer of some sort occurs. When force is applied, an impression is made or left on the surface. Those impressions can be cast and used as evidence to identify the object that made it. Casting impressions most commonly involve tire tracks, forcible entry, firearms, fingerprints, and impressions left on a body. All of these can be documented by way of photography, casting impressions, or actually taking the object or imprint as evidence.

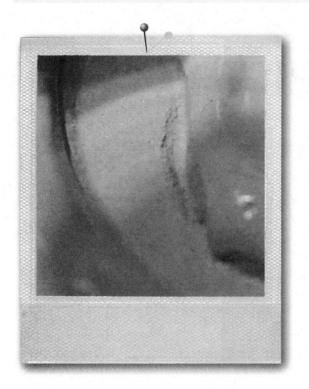

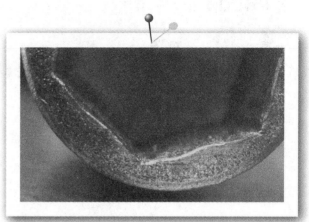

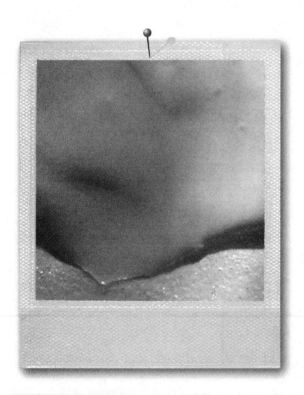

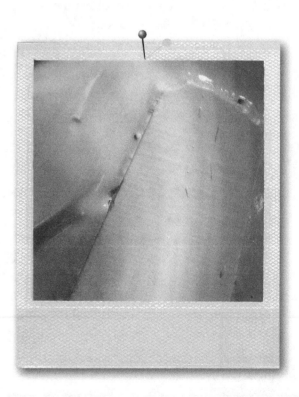

Tool Mark Analysis　　　　　　　　　　　　　　　　　　　　　　　　**147**

CRIME SCENE DO NOT CROSS CRIME SCENE DO NOT CROSS CRIME SCENE DO NOT CROSS CRIME SCENE DO NOT CROSS CRIME SCENE DO NOT CROSS CRIME SCENE DO NOT CROSS CRIME SCENE

Vocabulary

Blunt force trauma	Damage that is done to the body by a serious blow or blows from an instrument
Casing	An outer covering (for example, the sheath of a projectile or bullet)
Impression	A pattern, design, or mark made by something hard being pressed onto something softer
Microscopy	An investigation, observation, or experiment that involves the use of a microscope
Mikrosil	A fixative agent used for casting impressions
Projectile	An object that can be fired or launched (as examples, a bullet, artillery shell, or rocket)
Setting	The period in time and the place in which the events of a story take place
Striations	Patterning or marking with parallel grooves or narrow bands

Lesson Objectives (with Standards Guide Words)

- Students will learn what tool marks are and how they are made. (Guide words: evidence analysis, writing process, definition, application)
- Students will be able to create their own tool mark impression. (Same guide words as preceding objective)
- Students will be able to cast an impression using Mikrosil or Silly-Putty. (Same guide words)
- Students will learn the elements of a setting. (Same guide words, plus: literary analysis, setting)
- Students will learn how to develop a setting. (Same guide words as preceding objective)

Lessons and Learning Activities

Allotted time: twenty-five minutes

Using Mikrosil

Create a tool mark impression on a piece of wood. The softer the wood, the better. Use the end of a hammer or tire iron. (Other instruments can be used as well.) Strike the surface so that the face of the object is parallel with the board. This creates a nice impression in the wood. (Before the cast impression is made, look at the impression under the stereomicroscope. Students will notice striations in the wood or imperfections created from wear on the tool.)

Next, squeeze 1 to 2 cm of Mikrosil and hardener onto an index card. Use a wooden mixing stick to stir the two together. After it is mixed, which should not take more than ten to fifteen seconds, press the mixture into the impression. Do not wait too long because Mikrosil will begin to harden after approximately one minute. Let it sit in the impression for ten minutes at room temperature. When finished, remove it and look at it under the stereomicroscope. The resemblance should be easy to spot. If using Silly-Putty, examine the cast impression quickly because the Silly-Putty will retain its original shape. A hardener or fixative can be added to make it permanent. This can be purchased in any hardware store.

The Crowbar Catastrophe

Allotted time: thirty minutes
You need:

> One piece of two-by-four lumber, approximately twelve inches in length; use a crowbar and make an impression on the surface following the guidelines just given

Tool Mark Analysis

149

CRIME SCENE DO NOT CROSS CRIME SCENE DO NOT CROSS CRIME SCENE DO NOT CROSS CRIME SCENE DO NOT CROSS CRIME SCENE DO NOT CROSS CRIME SCENE DO NOT CROSS CRIME SCENE

Casting material (Mikrosil or Silly-Putty with a hardener)

Index card

Crowbar

Stereomicroscope

Camera if desired

On Saturday night, January 17, 2004, a shed was broken into that housed two all-terrain vehicles. The shed was made of pine wood. Since pine is a soft wood, there was an impression that seemed to show that some sort of bar was used for entry. Detectives arrived on the scene and made the quick assessment that most likely a crowbar was used. Detectives cut out a ten-inch section of the wood containing the tool mark. It was taken back to the station to be cast in Mikrosil.

In interviewing the owner, Mark Staton, the detectives learned that a man by the name of Russell McDonald worked with him at the steel mill. He was kind of rude and obnoxious. He also noted that Russell had been arrested before for stealing. Mark also said that he had been talking about his new ATVs and how much fun he and his son were having riding in the mud every weekend. Russell made a snide comment about how spoiled his son was and that Mark should stop bragging about his new toys. Mark shrugged it off and walked away. That was three days ago. Mark thinks Russell is responsible for what happened.

When the police arrived at Russell's house, he was working on his car. He slid out from underneath and asked why the two men were there. The detectives explained that they were investigating the theft of some ATVs. Russell looked down at the ground and denied everything. The detectives told him to relax, because they had not even asked him any questions yet. As the detectives looked around, they noticed a crowbar in the trunk of his car (the trunk lid happened to be open, because he was using the jack). Detectives said if he had nothing to hide, would he let them take a tool casting of his crowbar? To avoid looking suspicious, Russell agreed and went into the house.

The detectives made a cast impression and placed it in an evidence bag. They also took several photographs. Russell was nowhere to be found, so they headed back to the station. There they made a cast from the wood and compared it to the one they took at Russell's house.

Use the earlier learning activity; the impression from the wood and the crowbar in Russell's trunk will match.

150   *Partners in Crime*

CRIME SCENE DO NOT CROSS CRIME SCENE DO NOT CROSS CRIME SCENE DO NOT CROSS CRIME SCENE DO NOT CROSS CRIME SCENE DO NOT CROSS CRIME SCENE DO NOT CROSS CRIME SCENE

Springboard to Writing

Allotted time: fifty minutes

Setting is developed through describing the time, place, and location of an event. When movies are made, music is added to help establish the setting. It creates an atmosphere and sets the tone for the opening or a scene of the movie. Adjectives and adverbs are useful in developing a vivid image for a reader.

Ask students to think about how to develop a setting. After creating a list on the board, have students pretend they are the detective working on the ATV case. If this were to be the beginning of a short story, how could the setting really grab the interest of the reader? Have the students develop an atmosphere to get the reader interested in the mood that is created. Also, generate a small list of adjectives and adverbs that might be used in sentences. Ask students to create some sample sentences using the words on the board. The final product will be a page-long (single-spaced) introduction to a short story involving a theft of ATVs. You can also turn this into a full writing assignment. Use the assessment for grading.

CSI Notebook

Allotted time: fifteen minutes

Using the casts made in class, have students complete a short write-up explaining the differences between casts. For example, if two screwdriver heads have been cast, have students list the differences between the two. Also have them complete a short paragraph about why no two things ever are made, break, or wear the same way.

Assessment

- **Mastery (A).** Student writes one full page. Student uses illustrative adjectives and adverbs to describe the setting. Student creates a vivid image for the reader.
- **Proficient (B).** Student writes one full page. Student uses adequate adjectives and adverbs to describe the setting. Student creates an idea for the reader.
- **Satisfactory (C).** Student writes half a page. Student uses limited adjectives and adverbs to describe the setting. Student creates thoughts about the setting, but it is not a complete idea.
- **Unsatisfactory (D).** Student writes less than half a page. Student uses minimal adjectives and adverbs to describe the setting. Student does not create any ideas, thoughts, or images for the reader.
- **Insufficient (F).** Student writes less than half a page. Student does not use adjectives or adverbs to describe the setting. Student writes about ATVs or something unrelated to the topic.

Lesson Accommodations and Modifications

For students who are not sure how to use adjectives and adverbs in their writing, supply a list of such words for them to use. Also, model the correct way to use adjectives and adverbs by writing a sample paragraph on the board or on an overhead.

For Further Study

If students are interested in learning more about tool marks, they can purchase some Silly-Putty or Mikrosil. If they want to learn more about impressions, they can do research on a variety of surfaces, their density, and how easily impressions can be made in them. They might want to make some impressions of objects around their house. This might be a great exercise for students who like to work with their hands; it allows them to see direct results too.

A tool mark expert usually starts out as a detective. He or she has a bachelor's degree in criminalistics, chemistry, biology, or physics and one or two years of forensic laboratory experience in firearms and tool mark examination, using techniques specifically followed in forensic laboratories.

Cumulative Mystery

Allotted time: thirty minutes

> *At the lab, scientists received the picture of tire treads from the crime scene. The pictures were from the cars belonging to Jackie, Biff, and Magnus. The scientist then compared the pictures to the cast impressions taken from the crime scene. Which tire tracks belong to whom?*

For the teacher:

Take out three of the tracks from the crime scene. They should be from the cars belonging to Jackie, Biff, and Magnus. If you have not identified the tire treads yet, now is the time to do so. After the treads have been identified by manufacturer, they should be matched to the person. What happens is the first cast impression matches Jackie's car; the second, Biff's; and the third, Magnus's. This does not prove anything but it stands as circumstantial evidence. Cliff does not own a car, so there are no tire tracks for him.

There was also evidence of someone breaking through the door. You can prepare a piece of two-by-four with marks made from the claw of a hammer. Place it in an evidence bag, and then follow the directions for casting with Mikrosil. You should have three hammers, belonging to Magnus, Biff, and Jackie. The suspect hammer matches up with Magnus (connecting to his builder's skills). Perhaps it was left outside and the killer used it to break in.

152   *Partners in Crime*

CRIME SCENE DO NOT CROSS CRIME SCENE DO NOT CROSS CRIME SCENE DO NOT CROSS CRIME SCENE DO NOT CROSS CRIME SCENE DO NOT CROSS CRIME SCENE DO NOT CROSS CRIME SCENE

References

Adams, Thomas, and Krustinger, Jeffrey. *Crime Scene Investigation.* Upper Saddle River, N.J.: Prentice Hall, 2000.

Brown, Michael. *Criminal Investigation* (2nd ed.). St. Louis, Mo.: BH Security/Elsevier, 2001.

Conklin, Barbara G., Gardner, Robert, and Shortelle, Dennis. *Encyclopedia of Forensic Science.* Phoenix: Oryx, 2002.

Edwards, Martin. *Urge to Kill.* Cincinnati: Writers Digest Books, 2002.

Eliopoulus, Louis. *Death Investigator's Handbook: A Field Guide to Crime Scene Processing, Forensic Evaluation, and Investigative Techniques.* Boulder, Colo.: Paladin Press, 1993.

Fox, Richard, and Cunningham, Carl. *Crime Scene Search and Physical Evidence Handbook.* Boulder, Colo.: Paladin Press, 1987.

Genge, Ngaire. *The Forensic Casebook: The Science of Crime Scene Investigation.* New York: Ballantine, 2002.

Gerberth, Vernon. *Practical Homicide Investigation: Tactics, Procedures, and Forensic Techniques* (3rd ed.). New York: CRC Press, 1996.

Nickell, John. *Crime Science: Methods of Forensic Detection.* Lexington: University Press of Kentucky, 1999.

Chapter Twelve

Firearm ID and Ballistics

Overview for Teachers

Most people think of ballistics as identifying bullets and matching them to a gun. The actual name for that area of science is firearm identification. This means it deals with identifying ammunition and components of that ammunition as having been fired by a particular firearm that is unlike all others. Ballistics is the study of the motion of a projectile from the firearm. It also studies the trajectory and travel pattern of the projectile and how it affects its target. A specialist in this area knows physics and mathematics well.

Every bullet fired from any gun will have its own identifiable characteristics. Rifle and pistol barrels are produced by a process called machining. After they are machined, they are rifled. In this process, internal grooves are bored into the barrel of the firearm, intentionally to create a twisting and almost spherical shape. This gives the bullet a spin and creates more accuracy when it is fired. For the scientist, rifling makes each bullet as unique as a fingerprint. Some companies make firearms that are similar, but all are unique in some shape and form. Also, as the weapon is fired more, the barrel shows progressive deviations in the marks that are made on the bullet.

Attributes that make firearms unique are the number of lands and grooves on a spent bullet. Another is the impression that the firing pin makes when the bullet is fired. Yet another impression is created when a mechanism ejects the cartridge from the gun. All of these attributes can be used to identify a firearm.

At the lab, the gun in question has to be test fired. If the suspect bullet can be identified as to which company made it, then the same kind of bullet should be used in the test. The gun is loaded and fired into a tank of water. This slows down the speed of the bullet and allows it to land on the bottom of the tank without damaging it. It is retrieved, either by a gloved hand or by a pole with something sticky at the end. Again, this prevents any damage to the bullet. It is then placed under a comparative microscope. Both the suspect bullet and the test bullet are examined, and the scientist decides if there is a match or not.

The marks on a bullet are created when two objects forcibly contact each other. With a firearm, the marks are lands and grooves. Lands are areas that are indented on the bullet; grooves are the areas that stick out. This sounds backwards, but it is the gun barrel that causes these marks; therefore the lands and grooves in the barrel have the opposite effect on the bullet. There may be any number of lands and grooves on a bullet, from two to twenty-four.

In the case of shotguns, most barrels are not rifled, so they cannot be identified. Also, they shoot pellets and small BBs that are difficult to identify. Slug guns (shotguns with rifled barrels primarily used for hunting deer) can be identified as easily as a rifle or handgun. Most "sawed-off shotguns" do not have rifled barrels and cannot be identified. The point of sawing off a barrel is to give the gun a wider spread, meaning the pellets will disperse in a wider pattern at closer range.

To identify a shotgun shell, wadding is used for comparison. This plastic sheath is used to keep the pellets together in the shell. It comes flying out when the gun is fired.

Shell casings also have distinct markings (see the six casts from casing bottoms). Firing pin indentations are produced when the hammer strikes the primer and starts the reaction that fires the bullet. Some new guns, such as automatics, autoloading shotguns, and semiautomatic rifles, are hammerless, but they still possess a firing pin. Breech face markings are caused by the burning gases inside the bullet that force the cartridge against the back of the gun.

In automatic firearms, extractor markings and ejector markings are found. Extractor markings are made when the next bullet is loaded into the firing chamber. Ejector marks are made by the mechanism that flings the spent bullet from the gun.

All of these marks can be seen using a process called comparative micrography, involving use of a comparison microscope. This way a scientist can look at both specimens at once and match them up.

There are more in-depth ways to determine if a bullet is a match. They will not be discussed here because bullet samples might be difficult to obtain for a school. Since schools do not allow firearms (and rightfully so), you can obtain samples from the local police. Most departments have firearm training sometime during the year. Ask them if they can save some shell casings from their spent rounds. These can be looked at under a stereomicroscope; if your school has a comparison microscope, even better. Some teachers might have students who hunt or are sport shooters. You can request shells from those students, but let your school administrator know before you do so.

Mikrosil can be used to cast the tool marks on the cartridge. Using the same process as in the previous chapter, create casts of the bottom of the casing. These can be looked at for similarities and differences in the casts.

Introduction to Subject Matter

(to be read to students)

Firearm identification is growing in popularity thanks to advances in science. Experts are able to identify certain characteristics from one particular company and are currently working on identifying bullets by gunshot residue (with limited success). One misconception that people have is that ballistics matches up the bullets from a crime scene. This is not true. Ballistics is the study of the projectile and the physics involved in its trajectory, impact, and damage.

Vocabulary

Ballistics	The study of the travel pattern of a projectile and how it strikes a target
Breech face markings	Markings made when the cartridge hits the back of the gun as a result of exploding gases
Ejector markings	Markings made when the cartridge is ejected from the gun
Firing pin	A pin behind the barrel of a firearm that strikes the container of explosive (primer) to make the cartridge fire
Grooves	The indented parts of a grooved surface (for example, an indentation between ridges in the bore of a rifle)
Lands	The unindented parts of a grooved surface (for example, a ridge between grooves in the bore of a rifle)

Rifling	The cutting of spiral grooves in the barrel of a gun
Trajectory	The path of a high-speed object through space
Wadding	Plastic sheath material used to hold powder or shot in a gun or cartridge

Lesson Objectives (with Standards Guide Words)

- Students will learn the difference between ballistics and firearm identification and illustrate examples. (Guide words: evidence analysis, writing process, definition, application, comparison, contrast)
- Students will learn the areas of a firearm that make markings on a projectile or casing and illustrate examples. (Same guide words as preceding objective)
- Students will be able to identify breech face markings, ejector markings, firing pin marks, lands, and grooves and illustrate examples. (Same guide words)
- Students will be able to describe the process of rifling and what it is used for and illustrate examples. (Same guide words)
- Students will be able to identify wadding from a shotgun shell and illustrate examples. (Same guide words)
- Students will be able to find errors in verb tense and correct them and illustrate examples. (Guide words: past tense, present tense, future tense, evidence analysis, writing process, definition, application, comparison, contrast)
- Students will be able to find errors in noun-pronoun agreement and correct them and illustrate examples. (Guide words: nouns, pronouns, grammar)

Lesson and Learning Activity

Allotted time: forty-five minutes
For this lab, you need:

> Spent bullet casings of the same caliber (they should have been fired from three guns)
>
> Mikrosil kit or Silly-Putty and hardener
>
> Stereomicroscope
>
> Comparison microscope if available

Supply four bullet casings for each group. They should be placed in evidence bags. One should be from the crime scene; the others should be marked as coming from Stephen, Greg, and Jay.

158   *Partners in Crime*

CRIME SCENE DO NOT CROSS CRIME SCENE DO NOT CROSS CRIME SCENE DO NOT CROSS CRIME SCENE DO NOT CROSS CRIME SCENE DO NOT CROSS CRIME SCENE DO NOT CROSS CRIME SCENE

After students create molds (refer to Chapter Eleven for guidelines), have them use a comparison microscope or stereomicroscope for identification. (Stephen Wolf will be the match.)

This lab works in conjunction with Chapter Three. Rather than reproduce the story found there, please refer (for yourself and your students) to pages 59 and 60," reading through mention of Chapter Twelve and this lab, and then resume the lab here.

Who was the owner of the gun? Can it be determined if he was the shooter? How can police tell? Refer to Chapter Three for finding gunshot residue. The lab for GSR identification is there for this scenario.

Springboards to Writing

Allotted time: fifteen to twenty minutes

Working with Verb Tenses and Noun-Pronoun Agreement

Examine the next paragraph—a statement taken from a witness at the scene—to find errors in verb tense and noun-pronoun agreement. When a writer begins a writing piece, the tense is set in the first sentence and subsequent sentences should stay in the same tense (or shift to another tense using an appropriate transition).

Witness Statement

On Friday night, the humidity was setting in like a thick muggy fog. It was mighty hot and I was beginning to sweat. My watch said it is 9:15 and my head starts sweating. Then out of nowhere, these guy come driving by in his car and start shooting at us. His car is red and their license plate said gang banger, but it was shortened so it sayd GNG BNGR. I only seen the plate because I was laying on the ground to avoid the spray of bullets in the air. It was spraying all over the place. All I could hear is the banging and clanging of the bullets hitting things. When it was over, I got up and seen three people laying on the ground. Them guys were dead and I ran over to try and help them. They didn't move, so I figured they were dead. Then the cops came and they put crime scene tape all around. I was thinking it is weird that I was in the middle of that and I is alright now.

Corrections (Shown in Italics)

On Friday night, the humidity was setting in like a thick muggy fog. It was mighty hot and I was beginning to sweat. My watch said it *was* 9:15 and my head *was* sweating. Then out of nowhere, these *guys came* driving by in *their* car and *started* shooting at us. *Their* car *was* red and their license plate said gang banger, but it was shortened so it *said* GNG BNGR. I only *saw* the plate because I was *lying* on the ground to avoid the spray of bullets in the air. *They were* spraying all over the place. All I could hear *was* the banging and clanging of the bullets hitting things. When it was over, I got up and *saw* three people *lying* on the ground. *These* guys were dead and I ran over to try

Firearm ID and Ballistics

159

CRIME SCENE DO NOT CROSS CRIME SCENE DO NOT CROSS CRIME SCENE DO NOT CROSS CRIME SCENE DO NOT CROSS CRIME SCENE DO NOT CROSS CRIME SCENE DO NOT CROSS CRIME SCENE DO NOT CROSS CRIME SCENE

and help them. They didn't move, so I figured they were dead. Then the cops came and they put crime scene tape all around. I was thinking it *was* weird that I was in the middle of that and I *was all right* now.

Conflict Resolution Activity

Allotted time: two days

This is a good time to conduct a conflict resolution activity. Most students know that when gangs are around, there is usually some kind of conflict. Ask students about conflicts occurring at school. Generate a list on the board. Then spend some time talking about the situations, and have students share their stories. Also, stress with students that not all conflicts have a happy ending. Surely some students will share outcomes that have not been desirable.

Next, break students into groups of three or four. Assign each group a conflict that has been discussed in class. Have them develop a short skit of approximately two minutes in length. In their skit, they should develop a problem, climax, and have an outcome to the problem. Use the plan sheet below for each group.

Conflict Resolution Activity Plan Sheet

Create your dialogue here. Start off by assigning roles. One should be in charge of keeping the group on task, one to act as a recorder, another to get up out of his or her seat (for extra paper, to throw away trash, sharpen pencils, and so on), and the remaining members are contributors to the discussion. Use the area below and extra paper if needed to write out dialogue.

Task master:

Recorder:

"Gofer":

Contributor(s):

Allow one class period to plan and one period to perform. After each skit, stop to discuss each scenario. Have students relate their experiences to the scenario and suggest how they would solve the problem differently. While students are completing group work and presenting skits, you can use the assessment.

CSI Notebook

Allotted time: writing, ten minutes; classroom discussion, thirty minutes

Students should think about the impact that guns have on our society. This topic lends itself to much in-depth discussion. Ask students to write about one of these topics:

- Who has the right to own a gun?
- Who is responsible if a child finds a gun at home and uses it to commit a crime?

160 *Partners in Crime*

CRIME SCENE DO NOT CROSS CRIME SCENE DO NOT CROSS CRIME SCENE DO NOT CROSS CRIME SCENE DO NOT CROSS CRIME SCENE DO NOT CROSS CRIME SCENE DO NOT CROSS CRIME SCENE

- Who is responsible if that gun causes a fatal accident?
- What preventive measures should be taken by parents and adults to keep children safe?

Assessment

- **Mastery (A).** Student is aware of task and fulfills responsibilities. Student can clearly identify the conflict, climax, and resolution. Student actively participates in skit with high degree of activity.
- **Proficient (B).** Student is aware of tasks but is not focused for entire period of planning. Student identifies conflict, climax, and resolution, but not to the point of clarity. Student participates in skit with moderate degree of activity.
- **Satisfactory (C).** Student is aware of task but tries to do other tasks. Student can identify all but one among conflict, climax, and resolution. Student participates in skit with limited degree of activity.
- **Unsatisfactory (D).** Student is assigned task but is not focused and working with the group; causes distractions. Student knows the problem but nothing else. Student participates in skit with interruptions.
- **Insufficient (F).** Student causes constant disruption. Student has no idea what the conflict, climax, or resolution is. Student does not participate in skit.

Lesson Accommodations and Modifications

Students who are not proficient in understanding verb tense and noun-pronoun agreement will have difficulty completing this activity. Have students think about why people write correctly but talk differently. This has to do with learning how to use tense and pronouns correctly. Have students identify parts of the witness statement that sound the way they do when speaking. Chances are these are areas that need to be fixed. You should then discuss how to change verb tenses and noun-pronoun agreement. Complete the activity with students to model the correct way.

ESL students should complete this activity in their own language before attempting the English version.

For Further Study

If students are interested in learning more about firearm identification, they should contact the local police department for further information. Since this is not an area that is appropriate for school, have students work under the supervision of an adult.

If a student would like to be a firearms examiner, he or she could be a detective or firearm expert for the police station. Also, a degree in forensic science with a focus on criminalistics would suffice. On-the-job training in the lab is also necessary.

Firearm ID and Ballistics   **161**

CRIME SCENE DO NOT CROSS CRIME SCENE DO NOT CROSS CRIME SCENE DO NOT CROSS CRIME SCENE DO NOT CROSS CRIME SCENE DO NOT CROSS CRIME SCENE DO NOT CROSS CRIME SCENE

If interested in ballistics, he or she would need to study physics and mathematics because a lot of mathematical equations and physics are involved in figuring out trajectory and angles of projectiles.

Cumulative Mystery

Allotted time: forty minutes
You will need:

An evidence bag with the bullet casing from the scene of the crime

Two evidence bags with the two spent casings from the bar

Mikrosil

Index card

Comparison microscope or stereomicroscope

On Thursday night, Clifford Morrin was arrested at a local bar. He was highly intoxicated and got into an argument with another man about a pool game. They were ready to fight physically, but the bartender threw them out to fight in the parking lot. Five seconds later, the other man ran back inside stating that Cliff had a gun. As the bartender was dialing the phone, Cliff came back inside and fired two shots at the man, who was standing at the bar. Both shots missed and hit the wall. Someone came from behind Cliff and tackled him to the floor. On account of Cliff's drunkenness, it was rather easy for him to be detained until the police arrived, which was about two minutes later. Cliff was arrested and brought to the station for the processing he was growing accustomed to.

Back at the scene, police secured the area, cleared the room, and began their documentation. After photographs were taken, the two bullet casings were collected and the bullets were retrieved from the wall. They were then sent to the lab.

Students now conduct a lab on casting the bullet casing bottoms to those found at the scene of the crime. They will be a match and Cliff will be formally charged with attempted murder and the murder of his sister.

References

Baden, Michael. *Dead Reckoning.* New York: Simon and Schuster, 2001.

Burrard, Gerald. *Identification of Firearms and Forensic Ballistics.* Prescott, Ariz.: Wolfe, 1990.

Cooper, Jeffrey. *Art of the Rifle.* Boulder, Colo.: Paladin Press, 1997.

DeMaio, Vincent. *Gunshot Wounds: Practical Aspects of Firearms, Ballistics, and Forensic Techniques* (2nd ed.). New York: CRC Press, 1998.

Heard, Brian. *Handbook of Firearms and Ballistics: Examining and Interpreting Forensic Evidence.* Hoboken, N.J.: Wiley, 1997.

Ladenheim M. D., Jules C., and Ladenheim, Eric D. *Firearms and Ballistics for Physician and Attorney.* Chapel Hill, N.C.: Professional Press, 1996.

Nickell, John. *Crime Science: Methods of Forensic Detection.* Lexington: University Press of Kentucky, 1999.

Owen, David. *Hidden Evidence.* Richmond Hill, Ontario: Firefly Books, 2000.

Rinker, Robert. *Understanding Firearm Ballistics* (3rd ed.). Clarksville, Ind.: Mulberry House, 1999.

Warlow, T. A. *Firearms, the Law, and Forensic Ballistics.* New York: Taylor and Francis, 1996.

Zonderman, John. *Beyond the Crime Lab.* Hoboken, N.J.: Wiley, 1999.

Chapter Thirteen

Interrogation

Overview for Teachers

Interrogating suspects has been around for a long time. It still exists today and is of course always open to legal interpretation. The interrogation sometimes happens at the scene of the crime if a suspect is apprehended there on the spot. Other interrogations occur at the station after the police have acquired suspects for the case.

There are several methods with which detectives conduct interviews. In fact, teachers find themselves using these methods when interrogating students about a variety of events!

When interrogating a suspect who may be dangerous, it is essential to make sure that he or she is checked for weapons of any kind. Also pay attention to cues that the suspect might give to indicate nervousness. These cues should be noted by the person interviewing the suspect and recorded in the shorthand given here:

Break of gaze to right	>
Break of gaze to left	<
Clear throat	CT
Deep breath	DB
Delayed response	DR
Avoiding eye contact	AE
Grooming behavior	GB
Loud or obnoxious	!!!
Nervous laugh	☺
Fidgety	FY

Interviews can also be recorded for later use in the courtroom.

Before the interview begins, some basic information is needed. The suspect should be able to answer these questions without any hesitation:

What is your name?

What is your age?

What is your occupation?

164 *Partners in Crime*

CRIME SCENE DO NOT CROSS CRIME SCENE DO NOT CROSS CRIME SCENE DO NOT CROSS CRIME SCENE DO NOT CROSS CRIME SCENE DO NOT CROSS CRIME SCENE DO NOT CROSS CRIME SCENE

What is your financial status?

Do you have a criminal history or record?

Are you related to the victim?

After this information has been established, there are several ways of interrogating a suspect.

- **Alibi.** Ask the suspect where he or she was during the crime.
- **Narrative method.** Let the suspect tell his or her side of the story without interruption. The interviewer may use a tape recorder or video camera.
- **Question-and-answer method.** This seems to be the most common type of questioning. A question is asked, and the suspect answers while the interviewer records or writes the response.
- **Sweet-and-sour method.** This type uses two kinds of interviewers. One is nice and interrogates in a calm matter. The other is harsh in demeanor and approaches the suspect in an aggressive tone. This is also called the "good cop, bad cop" method.
- **Overheard conversation method.** This method is used when two or more suspects are involved. When the second suspect is interviewed, the interviewer tells the suspect that his or her partner has already confessed to the crime.
- **Bluff method.** This method is used to extract the truth from suspects. The interviewer says he or she is able to place the suspect at the crime scene thanks to witness accounts (that are made up). This method sometimes scares suspects into making a confession.

No method works better than any other. It depends on the suspect and how he or she responds to the method used.

As information is gathered, it should be organized in some manner. Information taken from witnesses also plays a key role in establishing the validity of the suspect's deposition (statement).

Introduction to Subject Matter

(to be read to students)

Interrogation of a suspect can yield important information. In some instances, the suspect admits guilt without even being asked. Others admit guilt when presented with evidence against them. Still others deny everything and lie. Suspects are sometimes foiled by their partners when the latter make a deal for a lesser sentence or some other attractive offer. Depending on the suspect, the response to the form of interrogation varies. Some do not need much pressure, while others will never admit their guilt.

Vocabulary

Alibi	A form of defense against an accusation in which the accused person claims to have been somewhere other than at the scene of the crime when the crime was committed
Bluff	To pretend to have strength, confidence, or the intention of doing something, in order to deceive somebody
Interrogation	The act or process of questioning somebody closely, often aggressively, in particular as part of an official investigation or trial
Narrative	A story or account of a sequence of events in the order in which they happened

Lesson Objectives (with Standards Guide Words)

- Students will learn the term *interrogation*. (Guide words: definition, comparison, contrast)
- Students will learn what an alibi is. (Same guide words as preceding objective)
- Students will learn numerous techniques for interviewing suspects. (Same guide words, plus: narrative, question and answer)
- Students will learn how to document interrogation by use of cues and questions. (Guide words: document interrogations, cues, questions, definition, comparison, contrast)

Lesson and Learning Activity

Allotted time: fifty minutes

By this point, as a teacher you will have developed a strong rapport with the local police department. Invite them in to give a lecture on how to interrogate suspects. They can share valuable information and add to the existing material in this chapter. They will also be able to give you an excellent demonstration of each method listed here. Remind students that some of the interrogation methods require raising one's voice; make your fellow teachers and administrators aware of what you are doing, so they do not come running or call the office.

After a lecture or demonstration, have the principal or disciplinarian of the building speak to students. How does he or she conduct her interviews with students when dealing with discipline problems? Students will notice it is not the same approach. At the end of the lecture, provide the following worksheet as homework; students can hand it in the next day.

Worksheet for Interrogation

- At what point in the investigation do the detectives interrogate suspects?

- What are some of the methods used in suspect interrogation?

- What are some of the cues that give away that a suspect is lying?

- What information is necessary before the interview is started?

- What method of interrogation does your principal use?

- How does it compare to those of detectives?

- Why do you think these methods are chosen by the principal?

- Why can't the principal use some of the methods detectives use?

Springboard to Writing

Allotted time: fifty minutes; three days for polished final piece
Here is a narrative essay activity that applies to the cumulative mystery.

> *That night at the police station, Cliff sat droopily in his cell wearing off his intoxication. Police wanted to give him some time to sober up before they interrogated him about the murder of his sister.*

Students should think about how the interview will be conducted. In a narrative essay, have students create the interview with Clifford Morrin and the detectives, using at least two of the methods that have been presented in this chapter. The students can decide if he will confess or lie. They should incorporate dialogue, and use adjectives and adverbs to describe the interview. The paper will be three or four pages in length (handwritten) when finished. Then ask students to revise, edit, and write a final draft for a grade. See assessment for grading.

CSI Notebook

Allotted time: fifteen minutes
Different kinds of interrogations require different kinds of personal qualities. What qualities does a person need to possess to conduct the various types of interviews listed earlier? The student should first list the method and then write what qualities that person needs and why they are essential to conducting that kind of interview.

Assessment

- **Mastery (A).** Student follows sequential order of events. Student provides a thorough questioning of the suspect through dialogue. Student has correct punctuation for dialogue.
- **Proficient (B).** Student follows sequential order of events. Student provides an adequate questioning of the suspect through dialogue. Student has minimal errors in punctuation.
- **Satisfactory (C).** Student writes about some events, but it sounds choppy. Student provides a sufficient questioning of the suspect through dialogue. Student has several errors in punctuation.
- **Unsatisfactory (D).** Student writes about interview and drifts in and out of the conversation. Student provides a limited dialogue. Student has many errors in punctuation.
- **Insufficient (F).** Student writes about the crime. Student does not use dialogue.

168 *Partners in Crime*

CRIME SCENE DO NOT CROSS CRIME SCENE DO NOT CROSS CRIME SCENE DO NOT CROSS CRIME SCENE DO NOT CROSS CRIME SCENE DO NOT CROSS CRIME SCENE DO NOT CROSS CRIME SCENE DO NOT CROSS CRIME SCENE

Lesson Accommodations and Modifications

Students who are not proficient in using dialogue will have a difficult time with this assignment. Using a T-chart, have them write "Detectives" on the left side and "Cliff Morrin" on the other side. They can write the conversation by using the chart. After each set of questions and answers are finished, ask them to draw a line showing the separation between the questions and answers. Then have them write their paper, without using quotes at first. They should concentrate on the spacing between paragraphs when using quotations. The punctuation can come at a later date, or in another lesson. This modification works well for ESL students too.

For Further Study

If students want to take this a step further, have them research other areas that use interrogation as a source of information (such as insurance fraud). Students should also consider that asking questions during an investigation is interrogation, but on a different level.

Cumulative Mystery

At the station, Cliff was pacing back and forth in his cell, yelling wildly that he had nothing to do with his sister's murder. He demanded from the police his one phone call. They escorted him to a payphone where he could make his call. No one answered, so he had to remain in his cell. The police told him that he would not be going anywhere because they had some questions to ask him. He said he would not talk to them until they gave him a cigarette. The police chuckled to each other and brought him into the interrogation room. They placed a pack of smokes on the table and asked him to explain where he got the gun. He said he had a friend buy it for him at a downtown gun store. Cliff knew he would not make it through the background check with his previous arrests.

The police then asked him if he was responsible for the murder of his sister. He looked at the detectives with glazed eyes, took a long drag on his cigarette, and said, "No."

The detectives then mentioned they had the bullet casings and they could be matched to the gun. They explained the process of how firearms are identified, and if his matched, he was finished.

Confused by the explanation they gave him, Cliff took a long puff on his fourth cigarette. He looked at the two detectives and said, "I did it. I was upset 'bout the money. That little bum got everything she wanted in life. I had to work and nobody respected me when I was a kid. Why should she have everything and I get nothing. Thas' all right, when I get out of jail I can have the money. I didn't mean to kill her. I just wanted to scare her into giving me the money. I broke into her house and waited till she got home. I just wanted to scare her so she would gimme the money."

The detective replied, "Well, I guess you don't know too much, Cliff. See, when you're taken off a will that means you don't get anything; even if you're the last surviving member of the family. The money goes to the state."

With that, Cliff threw his hands up in the air and started crying.

References

Albert, Joseph. *We Get Confessions*. Vancouver, B.C.: A.J., 1995.

Fisher, Ronald, and Geiselman, Edward. *Memory Enhancing Techniques for Investigative Interviewing: The Cognitive Interview.* Springfield, Ill.: Charles C. Thomas, 1992.

Fleisher, William, and Gordon, Nathan. *Effective Interviewing and Interrogative Techniques.* Durham, N.C.: Academic Press, 2001.

Inbau, Fred, Reid, John, and Buckley, Joe. *Criminal Interrogations and Confessions* (3rd ed.). Philadelphia: Lippincott, Williams, and Wilkins, 1986.

Interrogation: Techniques and Tricks to Secure Evidence. Boulder, Colo.: Paladin Press, 1991.

Rutledge, Devallis. *Criminal Interrogation Laws and Tactics* (3rd ed.). Incline Village, Nev.: Copperhouse, 1994.

Shuy, Roger. *The Language of Confession, Interrogation, and Deception.* Thousand Oaks, Calif.: Sage, 1998.

Vrij, Aldert. *Detecting Lies and Deceit: The Psychology of Lying and the Implications of Professional Practice.* Hoboken, N.J.: Wiley, 2000.

Walters, Stan. *Principles of Kinesic Interviewing and Interrogation* (2nd ed.). New York: CRC Press, 2002.

Zulawski, David. *Practical Aspects of Interview and Interrogation.* New York: CRC Press, 1992.

Chapter Fourteen

Crime Scene Re-Creation

Overview for Teachers

Before students begin to re-create crime scenes, they must understand the importance of having the correct details to re-create the crime scene as it happened. This can be accomplished through the use of developing a plot and setting.

Setting

The setting is where the story takes place. It includes such elements as location, time, date, weather, and surrounding environment. Elements of a setting are important because they describe the surrounding environment. If a crime scene is described as a house, what can we tell about the crime scene? Nothing. If we're told the house is in disarray, it could be a sign of attempted burglary or a struggle on the part of the victim. It could also represent a staged crime, which people do to make it look like a crime so the police won't suspect them.

Students should pay attention to the location of certain pieces of evidence. Why would they be in that particular location? Does the time of year or the weather have any effect on the crime scene? By creating a definitive surrounding environment, the investigator can establish a mental picture of the crime scene. This is helpful in piecing together the events that took place before the crime.

In some situations, perpetrators try to throw investigators off by staging a crime scene to cover up their tracks, as has already been mentioned. There are cases where the intention behind breaking into a house is assault. It is also common to see staging when a spouse is murdered for insurance money, or wanting to get out of a relationship, or to be with another person. Perpetrators go to great lengths to cover up their tracks.

The *modus operandi,* or MO, is how the criminal commits the crime. If a burglar robs a house and breaks in using a crowbar, that is the MO. The motive is the reason why the crime is committed. If the burglar is looking for jewelry, that is the motive for the crime. Along with MO comes a signature. This is a common pattern of behavior that the perpetrator will use. Let's say that a serial killer is on the loose. He ties up all of his victims before he kills them. He will use a certain kind of knot in each case. These will all be the same knot, because that knot is the one he feels most comfortable with. As he becomes bolder and more

172   *Partners in Crime*

CRIME SCENE DO NOT CROSS CRIME SCENE DO NOT CROSS CRIME SCENE DO NOT CROSS CRIME SCENE DO NOT CROSS CRIME SCENE DO NOT CROSS CRIME SCENE DO NOT CROSS CRIME SCENE

experienced, he might improve his signature by tying a new kind of knot that seems to work better.

Plot

After setting, the plot is the next important piece of crime scene re-creation. The plot is developed in three basic stages: conflict, climax, and resolution. The conflict is usually revealed in the beginning. There are many varieties:

Human versus human

Human versus animal

Human versus supernatural

Human versus himself or herself

Human versus technology

Human versus nature

These conflicts are usually followed by a series of events that lead to the climax. It helps to list them chronologically, to keep the crime scene as realistic as possible. After the climax has come to a head, it is time for the turning point or the resolution. How is the problem going to be solved? Students can use a form to select specific pieces from the police report to put everything together. Using a separate form helps organize data without shuffling documents.

Here are some possible crime scene re-creation questions:

- What is the conflict?
- Who is involved?
- What is the motivation?
- Where does it take place?
- What was the weather like on the day of the crime?
- How did the characters meet?
- When did they meet?
- What events led up to the crime?
- How was the crime resolved?

Introduction to Subject Matter

(to be read to students)

Piecing the clues of a crime scene together is a tough task. One needs to evaluate all of the evidence and circumstances before deciding how the crime occurred. The investigator needs to think carefully about placing events in sequential order to get a complete picture of what happened from beginning to end. This cannot always be done.

However, as an observer of a crime scene, an investigator must put together a report of what evidence was found and where it was in reference to other objects in the house. This report is eventually used in a court of law, so it had better be precise and correct or the defense lawyer will have fun.

Vocabulary

Climax	To reach the most important or exciting point in something such as an event or a story, or bring something to its most important or exciting point
Conflict	Opposition between or among characters or forces in a literary work that shapes or motivates the action of a plot
Modus operandi	How the criminal commits the crime
Motive	The reason for doing something or behaving in a particular way
Resolution	The solving of the conflict or problem
Signature	A pattern of behavior that the perpetrator will use
Staged crime	A method of feigning a crime to look like something else, to throw off investigators

Lesson Objectives (with Standards Guide Words)

- Students will learn the elements of a conflict. (Guide words: conflict, climax, resolution)
- Students will be able to identify certain events and categorize them into conflict, climax, and resolution. (Guide words: identification, categorize)
- Students will be able to form a paragraph, given a group of sentences. (Guide word: paragraph)
- Students will be able to identify and use parts of speech in writing a piece involving a crime scene. (Guide words: identification, nouns, pronouns, adjectives, verbs, adverbs, interjections, conjunctions, crime scene)

Lesson and Learning Activity

Allotted time: two days

Conversion of Details to Paragraph Form

Here is a list of details that can be put into paragraph form. The list could also be used as prewriting. Writers should take into consideration the organization of material in a sequential fashion.

List of Events

Monday, October 4, 2004

7:30 p.m.

Red fibers on shattered door

Broken lock on the door

Secluded house at the end of street

Police arrive at 7:33 p.m.

Drilled hole in safe

Stolen jewelry and television

Police are called

House is on a seventeen-acre lot

Dirt tracks in the house

Dressers overturned in bedroom

Walk into living room

Fingerprints on the doorknob to the house

Large piece of artwork ripped off bedroom wall, exposing safe

Smashed window on right front panel of door

Shattered glass on ground

Cigarette butt in the toilet bowl in the bedroom

Ask students to convert some of these details into a paragraph. The paragraph should follow a sequence that describes the events as they were discovered. Students should also use sensory details and descriptive words to create imagery in their writing. Since not all of the parts are available, students must fill in the areas where more information is needed to clearly state the process that is being followed. Here is a sample.

Re-Creating a Crime Scene out of a Scenario

On Thursday morning at 10:35 a.m., a police officer was driving up South Street when she noticed a house with the door wide open and a young infant playing on the porch. If the infant had been older, she would not have stopped, but something just did not seem right. She parked the car, went up to the house, and picked up the infant. As she stepped inside, she yelled out to see if anyone was home. After hearing no reply, she started to walk through the house. She noticed that the kitchen table was flipped over and there was trash strewn about the floor. Next, she walked into the dining room and found all of the plates and glasses from the glass cabinet on the floor. There were a couple pieces of silverware lying on the ground. Still there was no sign of a parent.

She continued into the bedroom, where the two dressers were flipped over and clothes were all over the floor. The officer heard something in the

Crime Scene Re-Creation **175**

CRIME SCENE DO NOT CROSS CRIME SCENE DO NOT CROSS CRIME SCENE DO NOT CROSS CRIME SCENE DO NOT CROSS CRIME SCENE DO NOT CROSS CRIME SCENE DO NOT CROSS CRIME SCENE

bathroom that sounded like running water. In the bathroom, the sink was running, and on the sink top was a toothbrush with toothpaste on it. The place appeared to be ransacked, as though being burglarized, but someone must have been at home because what burglar would stop to brush his teeth with someone else's toothbrush? The officer called for backup and waited for their arrival.

After students have identified the conflict, climax, and resolution, have them think about putting things back together. Even though not everything is revealed here, they can brainstorm ideas about what might have happened.

This scenario can be used as a springboard to a writing assignment. Students can fill in the missing details using adverbs, adjectives, and prepositional phrases. This crime scene can be re-created with detail to give more of a hint as to what really happened. Ask the students to think about what kind of clues could be discovered that might lead to some idea of what happened. There was no blood or weapons found at the scene, so students can exclude those materials from their writing. Students should think about trace evidence and where it might be located in the house.

Springboard to Writing

Allotted time: four days (split up over a month)
If an English teacher is currently teaching grammar, it can be incorporated into the writing process. In this case, have students complete the prewriting in three steps; beginning, middle, and end. Before this process begins, students can generate ideas about crime scenes. Write these ideas on the board for them to copy. Formulate the list along these lines (using the assessment in the chapter):

Kidnapping

Burglary

Bank robbery or "heist"

Grand theft larceny

Grand theft auto

Black market

Blackmail or extortion

Terrorism or bioterrorism

Identity theft

Computer hacking

Vandalism

Gang-related shooting

Drug wars

Arson

176   *Partners in Crime*

CRIME SCENE DO NOT CROSS CRIME SCENE DO NOT CROSS CRIME SCENE DO NOT CROSS CRIME SCENE DO NOT CROSS CRIME SCENE DO NOT CROSS CRIME SCENE DO NOT CROSS CRIME SCENE

The list allows students to choose a crime without getting into the blood, guts, and gore of crime scenes. If you are planning on having students incorporate elements of this kind, get permission from the building administrator first. It is very important for him or her to be in on all lessons.

Next, create a list for the point of view. This paper is written from a first-person perspective, so students will take on the role of their choice. Place a list of possibilities on the board:

Detective or police officer

Responding officer

Victim

Suspect

Perpetrator

Witness

Forensic scientist

Defense lawyer

Prosecution lawyer

Juror

Judge

Now begin to develop a plot. Create a list of events that outline the story from beginning to end. Once that is established, begin the writing process.

After the beginning has been written, students should underline ten nouns, circle ten pronouns, and put parentheses around ten adjectives. Have students hand in their work so you can check for understanding and provide feedback. You can also see if there are any parts of speech that might need remediation.

For the middle of the story, while students are completing the writing process, underline ten verbs, circle ten adverbs, and put ten more adjectives in parentheses. By using ten more adjectives, students have to include more details that help bring the paper to life. Students should hand in their paper for the same kind of checking as mentioned earlier.

As students write the end of the story, have them use ten prepositional phrases, ten conjunctions, ten adverbs, and ten adjectives. Collect the papers and check for understanding.

Eventually, students create a rough draft. When it is complete, ask them to go back and revise, edit, and publish. If you desire, quotation marks and dialogue can be incorporated into the paper.

You might find that students want to change their topic after they have written one section. That is at your discretion. It is usually beneficial, because students realize they have a better idea and have learned from their mistakes. Use the assessment for grading.

Crime Scene Re-Creation **177**

CRIME SCENE DO NOT CROSS CRIME SCENE DO NOT CROSS CRIME SCENE DO NOT CROSS CRIME SCENE DO NOT CROSS CRIME SCENE DO NOT CROSS CRIME SCENE DO NOT CROSS CRIME SCENE

Share these papers with the law enforcement officials and other professionals who have been working with students. This will truly make them feel like a part of the class.

CSI Notebook

Allotted time: two days

Now that the cumulative mystery has been solved, let the students go back and retrace the steps of the investigation. They should organize all of their notes and write a two-page story explaining how investigators made their way to cracking the case. They should write the paper in first person with the point of view of the detective. The first day should be spent on organizing information and the second day on writing.

Assessment

- **Mastery (A).** Student develops characters through use of examples and elaborate description. Student thoroughly develops plot and it is clearly defined throughout the paper. Student uses more than the required ten parts of speech.
- **Proficient (B).** Student develops characters with adequate description. Student develops a plot that is recognizable. Student uses the allotted ten parts of speech.
- **Satisfactory (C).** Student develops characters by using a list or chunking sentences together. Student develops a plot that is not clearly stated. Student uses fewer than the required ten parts of speech.
- **Unsatisfactory (D).** Student does not develop characters. Student does not have a plot that is developed; parts are missing. Student uses fewer than five of the required ten parts of speech.
- **Insufficient (F).** Student has one character who is not developed. Student writes about one part of the plot with no introduction or resolution. Student does not identify the parts of speech.

Lesson Accommodations and Modifications

Students who need additional work with parts of speech can ask you to guide them through the assignment. First, have the class pick one crime that they will all write about. Then let them choose their own point of view. Then model on an overhead the correct way to put together a beginning. Point out the parts of speech. Show students how each part of speech works with others to create a sentence; this gives them a better sense of what adjectives do, for instance. Repeat the same process for the middle and end. Also, limit the number of parts of speech that need to be found. Start with five and add on as students become more confident in identifying parts of speech.

ESL students should complete the activity in their own language. Once they feel comfortable identifying parts of speech in their own language, they can move on to English.

For Further Study

If students are interested in learning more about putting crime scenes together, they can do research on profiling of criminals. They also might want to look at a career in writing mystery novels. Students can write short mystery stories for extra credit and share them with classmates. Have students try to figure out whodunnit!

References

Conklin, Barbara G., Gardner, Robert, and Shortelle, Dennis. *Encyclopedia of Forensic Science.* Phoenix: Oryx, 2002.

Douglas, John, Burgess, Anne, Burgess, Allen, and Ressler, Robert. *Crime Classification Manual.* San Francisco: Jossey-Bass, 1992.

Douglas, John, and Olshaker, Mark. *Mind Hunter.* New York: Pocket Books, 1995.

Douglas, John, and Olshaker, Mark. *Journey into Darkness.* New York: Pocket Books, 1997.

Douglas, John, and Olshaker, Mark. *Obsession.* New York: Pocket Books, 1998.

Hazlewood, Roy, and Michaud, Stephen. *Dark Dreams.* New York: St. Martin's Press, 2001.

Lee, Henry, and O'Neill, Thomas. *Cracking Cases: The Science of Solving Crimes.* New York: Prometheus, 2002.

Chapter Fifteen

Court

Overview for Teachers

This chapter is the conclusion. Since the cumulative mystery has been presented throughout this book, it will be the basis for court.

Clifford Morrin has confessed to the murder and must now face a jury to determine his fate. You need to elect a prosecution and a defense team for court. (These terms were explained in Chapter Two.)

There needs to be a plaintiff and a defendant. The plaintiff in this case is the state; the defendant is Morrin. For this activity to work, it must be structured under your supervision.

People are also needed to testify in the courtroom. There should be two detectives, Morrin, and a forensic scientist. The detectives are named Bill Bretz and Glen Ragney. They will testify about these items:

> Evidence collection
>
> Taking evidence to the crime lab
>
> Collecting results from the crime lab
>
> Interviewing suspects
>
> Casting tire tracks
>
> Lifting prints
>
> Collecting the bullet casing and the weapon
>
> Collecting the hairs and fibers from the suspects
>
> Obtaining search warrants

The forensic scientist, Frederic Rieders, will testify about these items:

> Matching the tire treads
>
> Matching the fingerprints
>
> Matching the hair and fibers
>
> Matching the bullet casing and spent bullet to the weapon

180   *Partners in Crime*

CRIME SCENE DO NOT CROSS CRIME SCENE DO NOT CROSS CRIME SCENE DO NOT CROSS CRIME SCENE DO NOT CROSS CRIME SCENE DO NOT CROSS CRIME SCENE DO NOT CROSS CRIME SCENE

Clifford Morrin will have a prepared story that might look something like this:

> *I wasn't planning on killin' her. I just went there to argue with her and see if I could get some money outa her. She said she wouldn't give me any, so I took out my gun and threatened to shoot her if she didn't give me any money. I really wasn't gonna shoot her. She started to wrestle with me and the gun went off by accident. I didn't know what to do so I looked to see if she had any money sittin' around the house and she didn't, so I left.*

The defense will try to make it look like an accident and argue that Cliff should be let go. To do that, the defense has to carefully scrutinize the testimony of the detectives and the forensic scientist. Students must review information already learned and question whether the correct procedure was followed throughout the investigation.

You can conduct quick, ten-minute reviews of past lessons to refresh students on the correct procedure for evidence collection as well as following procedure and filling out appropriate paperwork. This review should take approximately one class period. Students can take notes to have a reference tool when they begin putting together their case.

Introduction to Subject Matter

(to be read to students)

Now that Clifford has confessed, it is time to take the case to court. The state is preparing to prosecute him for murder. The defense will try to get him off by saying it was an accident and the detectives and forensic scientists did not do their jobs properly. Using the past assignments and notes taken in class, prepare to seek justice for the dead Jackie or the unlikable Clifford.

Vocabulary

Cross examination	An interrogation of a witness or party to a case in a court of law
Defendant	The accused person, party, or company required to answer criminal or civil charges in a court
Guilty	Responsible for a crime, wrong action, or error and deserving punishment, blame, or criticism
Not guilty	Not responsible for a crime, wrong action, or error and not deserving punishment, blame, or criticism
Opening statement	The first statement used by the prosecution and by the defense, each to state its case to the judge and jury

Plaintiff	Somebody who begins a lawsuit against another person (defendant) in a civil or criminal court
Prosecute	To have somebody tried in a court of law for a civil or criminal offense
Testimony	Evidence that a witness gives to a court of law

Lesson Objectives (with Standards Guide Words)

- Students will identify the plaintiff. (Guide words: definition, comparison, contrast)
- Students will identify the defendant. (Same guide words as preceding objective)
- Students will understand the terms *prosecution* and *defense*. (Same guide words)
- Students will evaluate information on the basis of testimony. (Same guide words, plus: evaluate, testimony, evidence)
- Students will determine a guilty or not guilty verdict on the basis of testimony. (Same guide words as preceding objective)

Lessons and Learning Activities

Allotted time: five days

Day One

First, ask for a show of hands of who would like to represent the defense. Then do the same for the prosecution. If the sides are uneven by more than five students, elect some from one side to even it out.

Next, have students work in groups of four or five. Assign roles for each group member: leader, recorder, gofer, contributor(s). These roles should change daily, so every student has a chance to fulfill each role.

Students will also receive a worksheet. (See page 184.) Use it to write comments and give positive or negative feedback about the group. It will also be used later to formulate a grade. (You will have the most trouble with the last category: the group staying together and not interfering or disturbing other groups.) The worksheet is worth fifty points.

Students should begin by planning out who they want to testify for the trial. Once those people are established, they need to know what they will be testifying for and what information they will be able to provide about the case. People needed are two lawyers, the two detectives (Bill Bretz and Glen Ragney), the forensic scientist (Frederic Rieders), Clifford, Biff, and Magnus. Use the worksheet on page 185 for that task.

Possible Group Worksheet
(with roles and responsibilities)

Names:

Group assigns roles and tasks:

Group shares responsibilities:

Group stays on task:

Group sets goals and accomplishes them:

Group stays together and does not interfere with other groups:

Possible Questions for Mock
Testifying in Court

Name:

What is my background and experience?

What role did I play in the investigation?

What are my findings?

How did I come to these conclusions?

How can I explain my information to the jury so they understand what I am saying?

184 *Partners in Crime*

CRIME SCENE DO NOT CROSS CRIME SCENE DO NOT CROSS CRIME SCENE DO NOT CROSS CRIME SCENE DO NOT CROSS CRIME SCENE DO NOT CROSS CRIME SCENE DO NOT CROSS CRIME SCENE

Days Two and Three

Whichever role they choose, students should be thoroughly versed in what they did in the investigation, because the other side will be asking questions too. Students can now begin preparing a script that characters can use when testifying. Students should memorize their lines, not read from the paper. This will make the trial more realistic.

Days Four and Five

Since it is not possible to have all students represent Cliff or the state at one time (an option is to run two separate court sessions, to involve more students), groups are paired with one another, as prosecution and defense. The remaining class members are the jury. You, the teacher, are the judge. Students have one class period to conduct a trial for Clifford Morrin; the class will decide whether or not he is guilty.

The trial starts with the entrance of the judge. The prosecution follows with an opening statement and the defense does the same. After that, the prosecution can begin presenting testimony, which is subject to cross-examination by the defense. This process works vice versa for the defense too.

Students also receive an individual grade on their presentation to the class. Use the rubric on page 187 for this purpose.

This grade combined with the group grade will be out of one hundred points—fifty for the group grade and fifty for the individual grade. Students can see exactly where they gained or lost points. These rubrics should be shown and explained to students before the group work begins.

The last item of importance here is to invite administrators and others who have appeared as guests throughout the year. They will be thoroughly impressed with the amount of knowledge students have acquired throughout the year!

Suggested Rubric for Individual Grade

1. Student is prepared: _____ (10 points)

   Comments: _____

   _____

   _____

2. Student is aware of role in the trial: _____ (10 points)

   Comments: _____

   _____

   _____

3. Student presents his or her information with a thorough understanding that others find helpful: _____ (10 points)

   Comments: _____

   _____

   _____

4. Student shows self composure: _____ (10 points)

   Comments: _____

   _____

   _____

5. Student shows interest in assisting with the trial: _____ (10 points)

   Comments: _____

   _____

   _____

186   *Partners in Crime*

CRIME SCENE DO NOT CROSS CRIME SCENE DO NOT CROSS CRIME SCENE DO NOT CROSS CRIME SCENE DO NOT CROSS CRIME SCENE DO NOT CROSS CRIME SCENE DO NOT CROSS CRIME SCENE

Springboard to Writing

Allotted time: fifty minutes

For this writing piece, use the case of *The State* v. *Clifford Morris* as the scenario. Have students write a personal narrative from the viewpoint of a jury member. Why did he or she choose guilty or not guilty? In this writing piece, students should include the testimony of detectives and the forensic scientist. What was it about their testimony that made them believe Cliff was guilty or not? They should also think about cross-examination by the prosecution or the defense. Did they do a good job? What could they have done to strengthen their case? Students should have a one-to-two-page essay when finished. Use the assessment for grading. Students can also, throughout the process, make suggestions for improving the activity.

CSI Notebook

Allotted time: twenty minutes

Now that students have wrapped up their case, ask them to write a one-page reflective piece. They should evaluate themselves and the role they played throughout the process of the case. They should explain why they do or do not deserve the grade they received. (Obviously, students will need their score sheets back before writing this piece. This does not mean you will change the grade. They are recommending improvements to the activity.)

Assessment

- **Mastery (A).** Student is definitive in his or her choice. Student includes sentences about detectives, the forensic scientist, and the cross-examination. Student includes recommendations of how the activity could be better.
- **Proficient (B).** Student is definitive in his or her choice. Student includes sentences about detectives but not the forensic scientist, or vice versa. Student includes recommendations of how it could be better.
- **Satisfactory (C).** Student is not sure about his or her decision. Student does not use sentences about the detectives, forensic scientist, or cross-examination to back up his or her answer. Student makes feeble attempt at suggestions.
- **Unsatisfactory (D).** Student is not sure about decision. Student talks about reasons why he or she thinks Cliff might have been guilty or not guilty. Student does not address any suggestions.
- **Insufficient (F).** Student talks about the case and what part he or she liked about the investigation or something that is unrelated to the subject.

Lesson Accommodations and Modifications

For lower-level students, this activity might pose a lot of problems; there is a great deal of work involved. Start students off with an episode of *Law and Order*; do not show students the end of the episode. Wait until the writing assignment is finished.

Have them identify the plaintiff and the defendant. Also ask them to identify what testimony is and how it is used in court. They should also explain what a jury is and its job. After this is completed, students should write a two-paragraph essay explaining why the defendant is guilty or not guilty. Then show students the ending of the episode.

For ESL students, episodes are available in Spanish. This will make it easier for some students to understand if they are not comfortable with the English version.

For Further Study

Students who are interested in law and the art of arguing can conduct research on the Internet, or establish contact with lawyers who have appeared in the classroom.

If one is interested in becoming a lawyer, he or she must attend a four-year school and obtain at least a bachelor's degree. Then he or she must apply for law school, be accepted, and finally pass the state bar exam.

References

Ashworth, Andrew. *Principles of Criminal Law* (4th ed.). New York: Oxford University Press, 2003.

Braswell, Michael. *Justice, Crime and Ethics*. Cincinnati: Anderson, 1991.

Cordner, Gary, and Sheehan, Robert. *Police Administration*. Cincinnati: Anderson, 1998.

Gaines, Larry, Kuane, Michael, and Miller, Roger. *Criminal Justice in Action*. Belmont, Calif.: Wadsworth, 1999.

Gardner, Thomas. *Criminal Law: Principles and Cases* (3rd ed.). St. Paul, Minn.: West, 1999.

Peak, Kenneth. *Justice Administration: Police, Courts, and Corrections Management* (3rd ed.). Upper Saddle River, N.J.: Prentice Hall, 2000.

Wallace, Harvey, and Roberson, Clifford. *Principles of Criminal Law* (2nd ed.). Upper Saddle River, N.J.: Pearson/Allyn & Bacon, 2000.

Glossary

A	A human blood type of the ABO system, containing the A antigen
ABO	A human blood type of the ABO system, containing all three antigens
Acetate	A product made of or containing ester cellulose ethanoate; has a soft, crisp feel and silky appearance
Acrylic	A synthetic textile fiber produced from acrylonitrile
Adipocere	A soft, unctuous, or waxy substance, of a light brown color, into which the fat and muscle tissue of dead bodies sometimes are converted by long immersion in water or by burial in a moist place; it is a result of fatty degeneration
Adipose	Fat found in tissue just below the skin and surrounding major organs, acting as an energy reserve and providing insulation and protection
AFIS	Automated Fingerprint Identification System
Algor mortis	The temperature of a body after death, usually taken in the liver or the rectum
Alibi	A form of defense against an accusation in which the accused person claims to have been somewhere other than at the scene of the crime when the crime was committed
Alternative light source	A source that produces different spectra of light and is measured in nanometers
Amino acid	An organic acid containing one or more amino groups, especially any of a group that make up proteins and are important to living cells
Ampoule packet	A small sealed glass container that holds a measured amount of reagent to react with specific known illegal drugs
Annealing	The beginning translation of the DNA base
Artesian well	A natural water supply that can be tapped as a water source
Atomic mass	A unit of measurement that weighs the amount of atoms in an element
Autolysis	The first stage in decomposition, where anaerobic conditions are created and cells begin to breakdown
Autopsy	The medical examination of a dead body in order to establish the cause and circumstances of death

B	A human blood type of the ABO system, containing the B antigen
Ballistics	The study of the travel pattern of a projectile and how it strikes a target
Blanching	Term used in the process of lividity signified by a white area created by an object underneath the body, usually leaving an impression of the object
Blood typing	Any class into which human blood is divided for transfusion purposes according to the presence or absence of genetically determined antigens that determine its immunological compatibility
Blowback effect	The result of close or direct contact of a gun on the skin; tissue and blood particles appear in and around the barrel of the gun
Bluff	Pretend to have strength, confidence, or the intention of doing something, in order to deceive somebody
Blunt force trauma	Trauma caused to an area of the body from use of an instrument striking the body violently
Breech face markings	Markings that are made when the cartridge hits the back of the gun as a result of exploding gases
Cadaveric spasm	Instantaneous rigor mortis in the body, identified by clenched fists in a manner similar to the bench press
Cadet training	The training necessary for a person to become a police officer
Casing	An outer covering (for example, the sheath of a projectile or bullet)
Chain of custody	Establishing who enters the crime scene and handles the evidence
Charge	A fundamental characteristic of matter, responsible for all electric and electromotive forces, expressed in two forms known as positive and negative
Chromatography	A method of finding out which components a gaseous or liquid mixture contains; involves passing it through or over something that absorbs the components at different rates
CLEAN	Commonwealth Law Enforcement Assistance Network
Climax	To reach the most important or exciting point in something such as an event or a story, or to bring something to its most important or exciting point
CODIS	Combined DNA Index System
Cold case	A case that is never solved; sometimes with new technology, it can be reopened and solved
Conflict	Opposition between or among characters or forces in a literary work that shapes or motivates the action of a plot

Control sample	The standard against which the results are compared
Cortex	Located at the bottom of the hair; provides pigmentation for the hair
Cotton	A tropical or subtropical bush producing soft, white, downy fibers and oil-rich seeds (Genus: *Gossypium*)
Criminal justice	The study of the legal process of taking a case from beginning to end
Cross-examination	An interrogation of a witness or party to a case in a court of law
Cross section	A plane surface formed by cutting through an object at a right angle to an axis, especially the longest axis
Cyanoacrylate	A liquid acrylate monomer belonging to a group with adhesive properties, used in the process of fuming for fingerprints
DARE	Drug Abuse Resistance Education
Defendant	The accused person, party, or company required to answer criminal or civil charges in a court
Defense	The facts and their presentation as they relate to the defendant in a court case
Detectives unit	Police officers who are specifically involved with investigating any kind of crime
Diatom	A microscopic unicellular marine or freshwater algae having siliceous cell walls
Digested DNA	Fragments of DNA that have been cut by enzymes
DNA	Deoxyribonucleic acid
Document analysis	The process of determining whether or not a document is forged
Drug paraphernalia	Any device used to get drugs into the body
Ejector markings	Markings that are made when the cartridge is ejected from the gun
Electrophoresis chamber	Electrically charged chamber in which DNA separates itself
Entrance log	A list of all people entering a crime scene
Evidence transfer principle	Statement that any two objects coming into contact will leave a trace
Exhumation	The process of disinterring a grave so further tests can be run on the body or autopsied again
Eyewitness	Somebody who sees something happen and can give evidence about it
Fatty acid	An organic acid belonging to a group that may occur naturally as waxes, fats, and essential oils; fatty acids consist of a straight chain of carbon atoms linked by single bonds and ending in a carboxyl group

Firing pin	A pin behind the barrel of a firearm that strikes the container of explosive (primer) to make the cartridge fire
Flax	A plant with blue flowers that is widely cultivated for its seeds, which produce linseed oil, and its stems, from which the fiber to make linen is obtained (Latin name: *Linum usitatissimum*)
Fuming	The process of using cyanoacrylate to develop latent prints
Gastric content	The food remaining in the stomach after a meal
Grooves	The indented parts of a grooved surface (for example, an indentation between ridges in the bore of a rifle)
GSR	Gunshot residue; any residue that is left on a surface after a gun is fired
Guilty	Responsible for a crime, wrong action, or error, and deserving punishment, blame, or criticism
Homicide	A term used when someone is murdered
Hyoid bone	A bone found at the top of the vertebrae; a support or base for the tongue
Impression	A pattern, design, or mark made by something hard being pressed onto something softer
Interrogation	The act or process of questioning somebody closely, often aggressively, especially as part of an official investigation or trial
Ions	An atom or group of atoms that have acquired an electric charge by losing or gaining one or more electrons
KM test	Kastle-Meyer test; a presumptive test for all kinds of blood
Lands	The unindented parts of a grooved surface (for example, a ridge between grooves in the bore of a rifle)
Latent prints	Fingerprints that cannot be seen by the naked eye
Law enforcement	Any member of a police organization that deals with the laws governing a country
Leaking	The process of ink leaking out, creating a mark, usually a round dot, when a person stops or hesitates while writing
Lifeline	A rope that is secured to a diver when conducting a line search; the line is connected to someone on shore
Ligatures	Marks that appear on the skin from anything used to bind or strangle a person
Line search	A search that is conducted by setting up people side by side to search a suspected area for clues or a body
Livor mortis	The process of blood settling in the body after death; the color of the body changes depending on the time, temperature, and cause of death
Luminol	A reagent that reacts with the hemoglobin in the blood and creates a glowing effect
Mass spectrometer	An instrument used to separate compounds and measure their molecular weight

Medulla	The material that is located throughout the center of the hair
Microbe	A microscopic organism, especially a pathogenic species
Microscopy	An investigation, observation, or experiment that involves the use of a microscope
Mikrosil	A fixative agent used for casting impressions
Miranda rights	The rights that allow a person to say and do nothing until a lawyer is present
Mitochondrial DNA	DNA taken from the mitochondria in the cell; contains maternal DNA
Mobile phase	Components that become soluble and travel, leaving marks of separation
Modus operandi	How the criminal commits the crime
Molecule	The smallest physical unit of a substance that can exist independently, consisting of one or more atoms held together by chemical forces
Motive	The reason for doing something or behaving in a particular way
Narrative	A story or an account of a sequence of events in the order in which they happened
NCIC	National Crime Information Center
Ninhydrin	A spray that is used to develop latent prints
Not guilty	Not responsible for a crime, wrong action, or error, and not deserving punishment, blame, or criticism
Nuclear DNA	DNA taken from the nucleus of the cell; it is a fifty-fifty mix of maternal and paternal DNA
Nylon	A tough, synthetic material widely used in different forms in manufactured articles (for example, food containers, brush bristles, and clothing)
Opening statement	The first statement used by the prosecution and by the defense, each to state their case to the judge and jury
Patent prints	Fingerprints that are visible to the naked eye
Patrol unit	The officers who are out on the road and deal with situations as they arise
PCR	Polymerase chain reaction; it is a DNA replication system
Perpetrator	The person who is responsible for committing the crime
Pesticide	A chemical substance used to kill pests, especially insects
pH	Measure of the number of hydrogen ions in a liquid solution
Plaintiff	Somebody who begins a lawsuit against another person (defendant) in a civil or criminal court
Pocket	The separation of skin from tissue and bone due to the explosion of gases when the gun is fired in direct contact with the skin

194   **Glossary**

CRIME SCENE DO NOT CROSS CRIME SCENE DO NOT CROSS CRIME SCENE DO NOT CROSS CRIME SCENE DO NOT CROSS CRIME SCENE DO NOT CROSS CRIME SCENE DO NOT CROSS CRIME SCENE

Polyester	A group of condensation polymers used to form synthetic fibers
Polymer	A natural or synthetic compound that consists of large molecules made of many chemically bonded, smaller, identical molecules
Projectile	An object that can be fired or launched (as examples, a bullet, artillery shell, or rocket)
Prosecute	To have somebody tried in a court of law for a civil or criminal offense
Prosecution	The lawyers representing the person or people who are taking legal action against somebody in a court of law, especially the state or the people in a criminal trial
Pulmonary edema	A characteristic of drowning that creates a white froth coming out of the mouth and nose
Rap sheet	Record of arrests and prosecutions
Rayon	A fiber composed of regenerated cellulose derived from wood pulp, cotton, linters, or other vegetable matter
Resolution	The solving of the conflict or problem
Restriction site	The area where the DNA molecule is cut by the enzyme
RFLP	Restriction fragment length polymorphism; used for DNA replication
Rifling	The cutting of spiral grooves in the barrel of a gun
Rigor mortis	The progressive stiffening of the body that occurs several hours after death, due to the coagulation of protein in the muscles
Saponification	The breaking down of oils into very fine droplets called colloids; to hydrolyze a fat with alkali to form a soap and glycerol
Setting	The period in time or the place in which the events of a story take place
Signature	A pattern of behavior that the perpetrator will use
Slope	To be at or have an angle that deviates from horizontal
Smearing	A smudge on the paper left when a person drags the palm in ink that has not dried
Spent casing	The casing surrounding a projectile that contains the chemicals necessary to produce a reaction causing the projectile to be fired
Staged crime	A method of feigning a crime to look like something else to throw investigators off
Starring effect	A result from the tearing of skin from a close-contact gunshot; the opening looks like a star
Stationary phase	The absorption of material into the chromatography paper

Stippling	A result from a close-range gunshot; the GSR appears on the surface as little dots
Striations	Patterning or marking with parallel grooves or narrow bands
Suspect	To believe, without having any proof, that somebody may have committed a crime or wrongdoing
Testimony	Evidence that a witness gives to a court of law
Toxicology	The study of the nature, effects, and detection of poisons and the treatment of poison
Trajectory	The method of determining the path of a high-speed object through space
Victim	The person whom the crime has been committed against
Volar pads	The pads that eventually develop into fingerprints
Wadding	Material used to hold powder or shot in a gun or cartridge
Wool yarn	Spun from the short curly hair of sheep or other mammals; used in knitting or weaving

Other Books of Interest

Media Center Discovery: 180 Ready-to-Use Activities for Language Arts, Grades 5–8

Barbara R. Hamm

Paperback/ 400 pages
ISBN: 0-7879-6960-5

Using games and other innovative activities, *Media Center Discovery* encourages both student collaboration and the development of independent research skills, as well as critical thinking and problem solving. Useful in both school and public libraries, this book translates research skills into meaningful, fun, and personally fulfilling activities. Projects include: personal biography, story writing, and personal Web searches. Each lesson contains a concise and complete instructional guide for teaching a lesson in language arts or social studies, work pages for student practice, and suggestions for projects to encourage collaboration among teachers and media specialists. Lessons may be used in any sequence and students learn through the experience of doing the activities, followed by a final assessment or evaluation. *Media Center Discovery* is an essential tool that can be used to help elementary and middle school students learn how to locate and access information efficiently and effectively while becoming information literate.

Barbara R. Hamm has taught in both public and parochial schools for more than twenty-six years. She has been a classroom teacher, a computer specialist, and a library media specialist. Her professional credentials include a life certificate in elementary education and certifications as a learning resources director, library media specialist, and instructional designer.

Other Books of Interest

Listen to Learn: Using American Music to Teach Language Arts and Social Studies (Grades 5–8)

CD Included

Teri Tibbett

Paperback/ 464 pages
ISBN: 0-7879-7254-1

"Teri Tibbett's book will provide teachers with the knowledge, tools, and confidence they need to make music a part of everyday learning."
—Linda Rosenthal, violinist and professor of music, University of Alaska Southeast

Listen to Learn, with its companion music CD, offers teachers a dynamic way to use the history of American music to engage their students (grades 5–8) in reading, writing, social studies, geography, music, and multicultural lessons and activities. The book traces the colorful musical traditions of diverse cultures including early Native music, folk, blues, classical, jazz, country, Tejano, salsa, rock, and rap. The CD features authentic music from such American musical greats as Louis Armstrong, Woody Guthrie, Mahalia Jackson, Lead Belly, Lydia Mendoza, and many more.

Listen to Learn features a variety of fascinating activities that encourage students to write about their favorite music, investigate songs as poetry, research the lives of famous musicians, explore family musical traditions, research how instruments make sounds, plot record charts, and much more. Designed in a handy, lay-flat format for easy reproduction, the book is divided into four major sections:

Native American Music: Traditional Native American Singing, Traditional Native American Instruments, Native American Music Regions, and Contemporary Native American Music

European American Music: Colonial Music, Folk Music, Patriotic Music, Early Popular Music, Early Classical Music, and Instruments of the Orchestra

African American Music: Music of the Slaves, Spirituals and Gospel Music, The Blues, Dance Music, and Soul and Funk

New American Music: Modern Popular Music, Contemporary Classical Music, Jazz, Country Music, Latin American Music, Rock Music, and Rap Music

Teri Tibbett is a teacher and musician living in Juneau, Alaska. Since 1976, she has taught music at all grade levels, both as an itinerant music teacher and through her own school, The Juneau School of Creative Arts.

Other Books of Interest

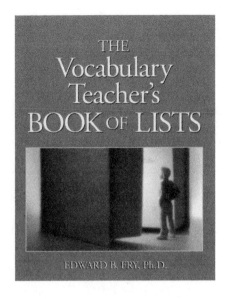

The Vocabulary Teacher's Book of Lists

Edward B. Fry, Ph.D.

Paperback/ 400 pages
ISBN: 0-7879-7101-4

"Teachers who want to mix test-prep with life-success-prep will welcome *The Vocabulary Teacher's Book of Lists* as an easy-to-use resource for lively lessons. They'll enjoy the wry humor of Dr. Edward Fry's teaching suggestions as he marries word work to wordplay."

—Lee Mountain, professor, curriculum and instruction, College of Education, University of Houston

The Vocabulary Teacher's Book of Lists provides content for literally hundreds of vocabulary improvement lessons for use by elementary, middle, and secondary school teachers, self-improving adults, home schoolers, and students studying for the SATs and ACTs.

Replete with lists of words, books, teaching strategies, and many other useful tidbits of information related to language and literacy, this book picks up where Dr. Fry's best-selling *The Reading Teacher's Book of Lists* leaves off. Its primary focus is on vocabulary improvement for reading and writing. It contains a comprehensive section on roots and word origins; extensive lists of words used in science, psychology, and literature; along with an entire chapter on vocabulary teaching methods and options for curriculum content. Other chapters include spelling, homophones, exonyms, affixes, and specialized subject area terms. With a wide variety of levels and lengths, some lists may be appropriate for individual students as extra credit; other lists will help ESL students to master English; and yet other students will use these lists to prepare for college entrance exams.

Based upon extensive scholarship and comprehensive references, Dr. Fry's *The Vocabulary Teacher's Book of Lists* bridges popular notions of vocabulary building and wordsmithing with the more formal academic study of language syntax and lexicon. It is an indispensable resource for both teachers and parents aiming to improve their students' vocabulary and literacy skills.

Edward B. Fry, Ph.D., is professor emeritus of education at Rutgers University, where for twenty-four years, he was director of the Reading Center. Dr. Fry is known internationally for his Readability Graph, which is used by teachers, publishers, and others to judge the difficulty of books and other materials. Fry was elected to the Reading Hall of Fame in 1993. He is the author of *The Reading Teacher's Book of Lists,* now in its fourth edition, from Jossey-Bass.

Other Books of Interest

Crime Scene Investigations; Real-Life Science Labs for Grades 6–12

Pam Walker and Elaine Wood

Paperback/ 288 pages
ISBN: 0-7879-6630-4

Turn your students into super sleuths with the 68 exciting lessons and labs in this unique resource! All provide complete teacher background information and reproducible worksheets that challenge students to observe carefully, think critically, conduct lab tests, document results, and try to meet the burden of proof to solve crimes ranging from check forgery to murder.

For easy use the labs are organized into four sections that will:
- Reinforce skills of observation, experimentation, and logical thinking.
- Help students identify unknown substances, recognize patterns, and determine the chain of events.
- Teach principles of inheritance, DNA analysis, and skeletal structure.
- Demonstrate how reconstruction of past events can influence the outcome of a criminal investigation.

All lessons and activities include complete background information with step-by-step procedures for the teacher and reproducible student worksheets.

I. **Critical Thinking:** Reinforce skills of observation, experimentation, and logical thinking.

II. **Physical Science:** Apply the principles of chemistry and physics to identify unknown substances, recognize patterns, and determine the chain of events.

III. **Life Science:** Focus on evidence left at crime scenes by living things and teach principles of inheritance, DNA analysis, skeletal structure, and characteristics of hair and skin.

IV. **Earth Science, Archaeology, and Anthropology:** Consider unidentified remains, mummies, skeletons, and more to demonstrate how reconstruction of past events can influence the outcome of a criminal investigation.

Pam Walker (B.S., M.Ed., Ed.S.) has been a teacher since 1981 and has taught science, biology, applied biology/chemistry, physics, and health and physical education in grades 9–12.
Elaine Wood (A.B., M.S., Ed.S.) has more than 14 years of teaching experience in physical science, biology, chemistry, physics, and applied biology/chemistry in grades 7–12 and has conducted research in genetic engineering.
Ms. Walker and **Ms. Wood** teach science at Alexander High School in Douglassville, Georgia.